Jean Kerus

CONFORMATION
FOR THE PURPOSE

CONFORMATION FOR THE PURPOSE

The make, shape and performance of the horse

SUSAN McBANE

SWAN·HILL
PRESS

First published in the UK in 2000
by Swan Hill Press, an imprint of Airlife Publishing Ltd

British Library Cataloguing-in-Publication Data
  A catalogue record for this book is available from the
  British Library

ISBN 1 84037 052 1

Typeset by Rowland Phototypesetting Limited,
Bury St Edmunds, Suffolk
Printed in England by Butler & Tanner Limited,
London and Frome

Swan Hill Press
an imprint of Airlife Publishing Ltd
101 Longden Road, Shrewsbury, SY3 9EB, England
E-mail: airlife@airlifebooks.com
Website: www.airlifebooks.com

DEDICATION

This book is dedicated to dear Rex,

my first 'ride', my friend and guardian

and the first dog I remember.

ACKNOWLEDGEMENTS

My sincere thanks go to artist Dianne Breeze for her unfailingly appealing and enlightening drawings which have now illustrated several of my books, to Elwyn Hartley Edwards whose inspiration this book was and to Peter Coles, my highly professional editor at Swan Hill Press.

PREFACE

Conformation, a horse's make and shape, has been the subject of fascinated attention and study by horsemen and women for thousands of years, ever since man realised that he could breed horses in whatever shape, size and way of going he wished provided he had the raw materials.

After horses were domesticated a few thousand years ago, man began noticing that certain makes and shapes of horse were better at performing certain tasks he had in mind for them than were others. This understanding of equine conformation was of crucial importance to early peoples and continued to be so until the Second World War because until that time horses were a major means of life-supporting transport almost all over the world. Choosing the right horse for the job could mean survival when your living depended on your horse being suited to the work you were asking; choosing the wrong horse could mean defeat, ruin and even death.

Millions of words must have been written about assessing conformation and some of the theories put forward have been based liberally on physics and mathematics, to the extent that readers without a maths-orientated brain could barely understand them. There have been complicated formulae of proportion, explanations of leverages, thrust, weight in relation to speed and various other ideas. And many of these theories, ideas and research findings have been soundly based and generally do work out in practice.

Research into equine biomechanics is fortunate to attract substantial funding in some countries (notably the U.S.A. and Canada) and continues today because of the increasing economic importance of the sports horse and racing industries. It helps us understand why some horses stay sound and others do not under similar circumstances, which horses will make the best showjumpers, dressage horses, event horses, harness racers, carriage horses and racehorses. But because every horse is an individual there will always be so many variables in each one, so many good and bad points, compensations and imponderables which affect a horse's performance, that the subject will never be truly 'cracked' and will retain its fascination far into the unforseeable future.

One thing is certain: good conformation is by no means guaranteed to make a good mover or a good athlete, surprising though that may seem. We may have a better chance of getting what we are looking for and of that horse remaining sound (given a normally strong constitution, good training, correct riding or driving and appropriate management for both the horse and his job), but there are many swans which suddenly turn into camels in motion – and many stationary camels which consistently win major prizes.

Temperament, 'heart', mood and inclination have a great deal to do with how a horse works but are outside the scope of this book. So does his musculature (its type and function) and his nervous system, which 'fires' the muscles in the first place. His physical action, which is governed by his skeletal structure, his muscles and his nervous efficiency, is obviously vital to his performance, as is whether or not he stays sound under the pressure of work. Handsome certainly is as handsome does. That is why this book is not simply a dry textbook about horses standing still but takes in – in addition to the horse's physical structure and appearance – his action, the stresses this places on his body and the importance of correct training for movement. The title of the book is *Conformation for the Purpose* and different makes, shapes, types and conformational features are considered in relation to the job their owner is expected to perform.

Because so many people find complicated conformational formulae expressed in terms of maths and physics difficult, if not impossible, to understand, I have purposely tried to keep the book fairly simple but accurate, without 'dumbing down' the subject, as seems to be the fashion these days. I hope the result is a clear overview of the whole topic of conformation, action and performance related to horses' varied jobs, presented in a way which readers will find informative, interesting and understandable.

SUSAN McBANE

CONTENTS

1

HOW HORSES DEVELOPED

When we look around at the vast variety of horses and ponies that are members of the species of the domesticated horse, *Equus caballus*, it is hard to imagine that they all stem from an ancestor no bigger than a fox and looking nothing at all like a horse. In fact, when the fossils of this little forest-dwelling animal were first discovered in deposits from the Eocene (about 54–38 million years ago), it was named *Hyracotherium* because the shape of its skull made palaeozoologists think it was related to the hyrax (*Procaviidae*), a land- or tree-living herbivore which looks not unlike a rabbit.

When more fossils were found later by different people, the species was recognised as a horse type (as it turned out, the earliest direct horse ancestor) and so was named *Eohippus* – *hippus* being from the Greek *hippos* for 'horse' and *eo* from Eocene, which itself is from the Greek *eos* meaning 'dawn' and *kainos* meaning 'new'. For this reason, *Hyracotherium/Eohippus* is also called, in more user-friendly terms to most of us, the Dawn Horse.

The Eocene is so called because it was the dawning of the rise of the mammals after many millions of years of domination by reptiles, notably dinosaurs. Their demise freed many evolutionary niches for other species and little shrew-like mammals, among many other types of animals, made good use of it. Prior to the Eocene, there were Condylarths, an unspecialised group of mammals, some more like insectivores but others having five-hooved toes and the beginnings of grazing-type teeth. From them

developed all ungulates – large, hoofed, grazing mammals. It is easy to think of evolution as a direct line, one species leading to another to another down to the present day, but this is not at all how it is. Evolution *can* be like this, with species not changing for long periods or changing steadily, but it can also occur in fits and starts for reasons such as:

- changes in climate which might affect the type of vegetation, which in turn might or might not be suitable for existing animal species as a food supply
- suitable breeding and living habitat
- evolving disease organisms
- the general environment
- predation by other species
- the invasion of habitat by other species

These factors all alter the survival chances of a particular organism.

These sorts of events have made many species extinct and continue to do so today, although now man, *Homo sapiens*, a relative newcomer to the scene, is the prime cause of extinctions which are occurring much faster than at any time in the earth's history. It is man who has caused the horse and some of its relatives to become extinct in the wild and brought other equine types such as Grévy's Zebra, the Cape Mountain Zebra, the Asiatic Wild Ass, the Przewalski Horse and the Exmoor Pony to dangerously low levels by hunting them and taking or polluting their habitat.

The horse's place

The horse's place amongst the domesticated animals is unique. Man domesticated animals, obviously, because he felt he could make use of them to enhance his chances of survival and prosperity. Primitive families, groups or tribes first hunted the ancestors of our present horses for food, hide, hair, blood and bone. Even horn and teeth were made use of, mainly in the making of jewellery. As domestication occurred, mares also supplied milk and early peoples gradually began to appreciate the qualities of both strength and speed in the horse, for traction, pack work and riding.

Combined with its general 'trainability', these made the horse the most useful all-round animal man could want. The camel can go longer without water and has speed, but most are unpleasant by nature, not exactly beautiful to look at, uncomfortable to ride compared with the horse and nothing like as strong as horses when it comes to draught use.

The dog, of course, is traditionally known as 'man's best friend', although animal charities would all disagree with that; recent figures showed that, on a percentage basis calculated from species numbers, the dog is the most abused animal in the world, with equines coming next. The dog often spends more time with humans than the horse and often lives in the family home, unlike horses. It is also noted for great fidelity, even to cruel owners, unlike the horse which is definitely inclined to bear grudges. But of course the dog does not have the strength of the horse and cannot be ridden, although dogs are used for light draught work such as in sleds, and larger breeds for pulling light carts for deliveries. All round, however, the horse is by far man's most useful animal ally.

Characteristics ancient and modern

Where did the qualities come from for which we value the horse? What qualities did *Hyracotherium* have and do any of them exist in today's horses? What did *Hyracotherium* look like and how did it behave?

The environment in the northern hemisphere in the Eocene was swampy, dense, tropical forest, nothing like the grassy plains or the steppe and tundra for which today's horses are fitted. *Hyracotherium* was about fox-sized, with an arched and much more flexible spine than its descendant *Equus*, enabling it to twist and turn in its dense forest environment. This spine involved a much more flexible lumbar (loin) region and a short neck. The teeth, of which it had more than its descendant, included larger, functional canine teeth or tushes possibly used for tearing into large, tougher fruits, but were otherwise smaller and weaker than the horse's, being mainly suited to eating leaves and soft fruits from shrubs, low-hanging tree branches and ground-growing plants. Grasses, which were much tougher and abrasive, had not yet evolved.

Its limbs and feet were different, too. The forearm bones, the radius and ulna, were separate as they are in humans, which made the leg less stable as a weight-bearing structure but able to rotate and twist, unlike the leg of the modern horse which moves in a single, forward-backward plane. The hindlegs were proportionately longer than in the modern horse, making the Dawn Horse and several of its descendant species croup high and good at rapid standing starts and at jumping over obstacles on the crowded and overgrown forest floor, such as fallen tree trunks, tussocks, branches, large surface roots, gulleys and the like. The feet were like the paws of a dog, with blunt claws on toes. It had four toes on its forefeet and three on its hind, each with pads, and a larger central pad behind them. The lower legs, too, had not elongated as they did in later descendants, a feature which facilitated the development of speed.

On the whole, then, *Hyracotherium* was well suited to its forest environment. It was able to escape predators by getting off to a rapid start, jumping whatever obstacles it met in its path and twisting in and out of the undergrowth and tree trunks. The features of its family life are not clear – whether it lived singly, in pairs or, as seems likely, in family groups – but it would have made good use of the ample hiding places in a dense forest and was probably assisted by the camouflage offered by dapples, spots, stripes and colour patches on the coat.

Some of the qualities mentioned above are clearly present in today's horses, even down to dapples and colour patterns. The instinct to run from danger is uppermost in the mind of even the most well-trained and disciplined horse and also, in some horses and ponies, the desire to hide when possible. Many horses and ponies have an obviously natural jumping ability and all of them retain the inherent escape mechanism of the standing start which takes modern horses from dozing to a maximum of 70 k.p.h. (45 m.p.h.) in less than four or five seconds, regardless of breed or type.

The main changes which affected the speed of today's horses and their inclination towards straight-line flight were:

- *The flattening out of the spine*. The main bodies of the vertebrae in the modern horse's spine still form a slight arch and the back, at high speeds, is held down and firm by the longissimus dorsi muscles, among others, which run the length of the back.
- *The development of the spinous processes or upper bony projections of the vertebrae in the wither area.* This stabilised the neck and provided an increased facility for muscle attachment.
- *The lessening of sideways flexibility in the loin or lumbar section of the spine*. This resulted from changes in the structure of the vertebrae and the fact that their transverse processes (projecting sideways) began to articulate (become joined) as well as their main bodies, allowing for up-and-down flexion but not sideways flexion.
- *The fusing of the forearm bones, radius and ulna.* This gave greater stability and strength under the stress of speed whilst restricting the movement of the leg to a forward-backward swing. The fibula and tibia are also fused in the modern horse, forming the gaskin or second thigh bone between stifle and hock; the hindleg, like the fore, swings in a forward-backward plane but, owing to the elongated ball-and-socket hip joint, slight

sideways movement is possible – although nothing like as much as some farriers seem to think!
- *The lengthening of the lower legs, particularly the forelegs*. There was also a reduction in the number of toes.
- *The change of environment*. Swampy forests, in which headlong flight was impossible, gave way to open plains, on which it was very much the thing to do to escape predators, there being no dense forest to hide in and plenty of room to run flat out in a straight line.

Changing descendants

Hyracotherium seems to have been a very successful species in its own right. Although very primitive by horse standards, it was an advanced, specialised mammal in the animal world of the time, well along the evolutionary path. Its fossils have been found in its acknowledged 'birthplace', the Americas, but also in Europe to where it probably migrated across the widening swamp which was to become the Atlantic. *Hyracotherium* was probably about 60 cm (24 in) at the withers and there were several types often surviving at the same time.

In fact, the 'tree' of evolution shows that several horse ancestors (even though they may not have been recognisable to us as horses) lived for long periods at the same time. Of course, one type did not suddenly disappear and another take its place: some changed and possibly interbred with others, many died out and some progressed until today the only descendant of *Hyracotherium* is *Equus*, of which we have three main types: horses, asses and zebras.

Basically, species can only change because of genetic mutation or alteration. Genes are passed on to offspring in equal numbers from each parent but some are termed 'dominant' and some 'recessive'. Genes are responsible for all an organism's characteristics but those characteristics which are noticeable or 'expressed' come from dominant genes and those which the organism still carries but which are not expressed come from recessive genes. An organism may carry on unchanged for many millions of years (for example, bees and crocodiles) and may suddenly change relatively quickly, or there may be spurts of change, or change may be more gradual.

Creatures developing in a given environment must have the appropriate characteristics to enable them to survive in that environment (for example, most fish cannot live long out of water) but if their environment changes to the extent that those features no longer enable them to live in it, the species dies out – unless its genes mutate and produce different features which enable it to cope in different surroundings.

As far as horse ancestors are concerned, chance genetic mutations occurred in many types which enabled them to adapt to the earth's changing environment. The appearance of grasses, plains and similar environments were met, by *Hyracotherium* and its descendants, with increased size, a flatter, less flexible spine (one of the features which facilitated speed), a longer neck and head to reach down to graze these new plants from atop longer legs, larger, stronger teeth to cope with those grasses, a fusing of upper leg bones, a considerable lengthening of the lower legs and a reduction in the number

of toes which ideally fitted the ultimate horse family for galloping on grassy turf.

There is a school of thought which believes that change in a species is driven by the environment, i.e. that organisms somehow sense that change is needed and produce different features to meet it. Most scientists involved and interested in evolution, however, believe that it is purely chance mutations which cause a species to adapt and to survive and be fitted for a changing environment; the expression 'survival of the fittest' actually means 'survival of the most suitable'. This is one reason why, over millions of years, so many species which did not undergo such chance mutations died out and why evolution on the whole takes such a very long time. Members of those species which do not experience genetic change and the development of features which better fit it to survive in a new or changing environment will not survive to breed and pass on their own, no longer suitable, genes. Those which do develop more suitable features survive longer and may breed, and so pass on those genes to their offspring. In nature, animals born with significant defects either die or are killed off, preventing those

The equine species evolved specifically as grazing, running animals with rapid standing starts as a speciality, able to reach top speed in about four seconds, due to the exigencies of predation. As a matter of interest, the zebra's and horse's top speed is slightly more than half that of the cheetah but if the equines can get a good start by setting off before the predator gets close enough their superior stamina usually wins the day. A single cheetah is not strong enough to bring down and kill an adult zebra but will often go for youngsters

defects which are genetic from being passed on. Therefore, only the best fitted to their environment have a chance to propagate the species. This is natural selection in action – the environment selects the fittest.

The new, much more open environment also led to the development of a strong herding instinct in most modern horse types, the flight-or-fight instinct mainly in horses and zebras and their famous standing starts, which are used so successfully by man in sprint racing, polo, show-jumping against the clock and cutting cattle. The horse's stamina was also developed more and more as he became able to stay ahead of most of his predators, this being one of his most attractive features to man.

After *Hyracotherium* which, as we have seen, lived mainly during the Eocene from about 54 to 38 million years ago, a main descendant was *Mesohippus*, which lived during the Oligocene roughly 38 to 26 million years ago. It was larger and continued to browse from trees and shrubs but could also eat the developing grasses and had bigger teeth and a bigger head to accommodate them. Although still multi-toed, its side toes bore little weight except at speed. It would have been developing the instinct to run as well as to hide. All these features were even more advanced in its descendant, *Miohippus*.

During the Miocene (approximately 24 to 5 million years ago), several types developed, such as *Parahippus*, *Merychippus* (whose side toes were present but not functional) and *Pliohippus*. The latter would have been immediately recognisable to us as a horse type with its horse-like back and body, neck, head and single-toed feet (although some of its variants have been found with small side toes). The animal now generally regarded as the true, immediate and direct ancestor of *Equus* lived from about 12 to 4 million years ago and is called *Dinohippus*. About the size of a small pony, it had large, strong teeth and powerful jaw muscles to grind up the tough grasses and usually had no side toes at all.

Then, at last, came *Equus* and its variants. It was about 1.4 m (54 in) tall at the withers, or about 13.2 hands high in horse-talk, had the familiar single-toed, tough hoof, large and very

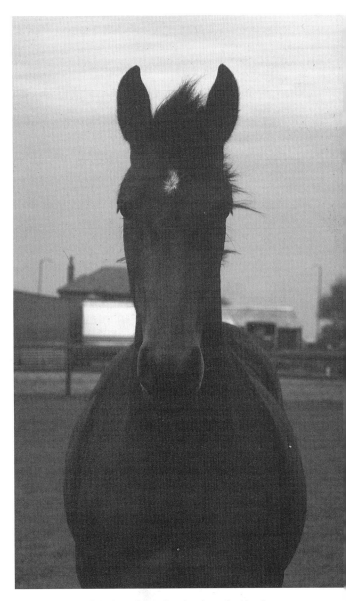

The structure of the horse's head makes it perfect for detecting predators. The ears can each move virtually 180 degrees to detect sounds from any direction, directing sound waves down the well-developed, curved pinna (the only part of the ear we can see). The eyes are placed on the extreme sides of the head so that the horse can see almost all around him without moving the head at all. To see directly behind him, all he has to do is move the head very slightly to one side. The head is also long enough to raise the eyes above the length of most grasses so that the horse can see all around him most of the time whilst grazing. The nostrils are capable of expanding greatly to take in the smells of predatory animals. When the wind is in the right direction, it is believed that horses can detect smells up to a mile away

strong teeth and a well-developed herding and flight instinct. The spine was truly horse-like and restricted in lateral flexibility but beautifully equipped for straight-line flight, which has always been the horse's first line of defence.

The horse (and, of course, the ass and the zebra) had arrived.

Spread and development

The development of the horse types over millions of years was significantly affected by other changes occurring on the earth. The development of land masses, their movements – breaking up and colliding – the creation and destruction of land bridges, the appearance of mountain ranges as huge plates of land collided and pushed up the earth and the appearance of seas and lakes as they pulled apart, the eroding out of glacial basins and river valleys, the appearance of oceans, forests, plains, steppes, tundras and deserts repeatedly opened up and closed migration routes for all animals. Groups of animals travelled or were cut off, moved on again and became trapped as the earth changed. The rising and falling of sea levels, the coming and going of ice ages and the emergence of climate and weather systems all decided where horses (and, of course, all other organisms) spread to, where they stayed, what climate they experienced in any given place and, therefore, what physical features they developed.

Although horses have always been prey animals, a circumstance which has governed their psychological qualities (run first and maybe think later), their diverse physical types have evolved for physical reasons of climate and terrain and of gene-pool availability and mutation. The resulting types of horse and pony became quite incidentally useful to man because of their different conformations and propensities.

From roughly 10 to 5 million years ago, during the late Miocene, there were as many as sixteen different horse types but, for any of the various reasons already given, only one, *Dinohippus*, survived and gave rise to *Equus*. Even then, the future of horses was by no means

assured: for reasons which are still speculated upon, *Equus* itself died out in its homeland, North America, only 10,000 years ago – a tiny blip in the timescale of evolution – and survived only in Eurasia and (asses and zebras only) Africa. The last Ice Age had ended gradually about 10,000–12,000 years ago and it is calculated that the horse was reduced to a mere few thousand individuals spread thinly over Eurasia.

Most researchers and workers in the fields of palaeozoology, evolution and related areas believe that by the end of the last Ice Age there had developed three main types of natural, primitive horse and pony.

The first was the *Forest* or *Diluvial Horse*, which is popularly regarded as massive, ugly, slow, stupid and extremely hardy. It may well have been phlegmatic, super-chunky and tough but this does not mean that it was stupid (otherwise it would not have had the wit to survive) and it was certainly not big in modern terms, like heavy draught horses. In fact, the romantic myth of knights in shining armour going into battle mounted on chargers of Shire Horse dimensions is exactly that – a myth. Although the Forest Horse is believed to have given rise to all the heavy breeds and so is a principal ancestor of all modern competition warmbloods and others, it is interesting to note that until about AD 1500 there were no horses taller than about 15 hands high. The increased height was produced by man's improving knowledge of selective breeding – artificial as opposed to natural selection.

The Forest Horse seems to have developed mainly in the cold, wet forests of what became eastern Europe. It would have had thick, coarse hair and 'dinner plate' feet to help it cope with the boggy ground and produced several variants before becoming extinct or being absorbed into them. Although the Forest Horse itself is extinct, its characteristics, mentality and physical features can still be found in its many descendants.

The second type is still with us and, thanks to dedicated work by conservationists, is increasing in numbers, having been brought back from the very brink of extinction, unlike so very many of its predecessors. This is the *Asiatic* or *Mongolian Wild Horse* also known as the *Przewalski Horse*. Its natural home, the tundra and steppe of northern and eastern Asia, saw its reintroduction to the wild during the last decades of the twentieth century and this project is continuing. Groups are also living 'wild' (ferally) in Europe and the U.S.A. and there are other breeding groups in safari parks, reserves, zoos and private collections. Because today's population has been built up from a mere handful of individuals rescued from the wild, where they were being hunted and preyed upon, and represents a tiny gene pool, each mating is carefully controlled by a central administrative body at Prague Zoo to ensure that closely related individuals are not mated together.

The Przewalski Horse is famous because of its precarious situation as regards numbers (there are now around 1000), its different number of chromosomes from all other horses and ponies (it has sixty-six instead of sixty-four) and its characteristic upright mane with no forelock. It is extremely resistant to cold, harsh weather and lives in sub-zero temperatures for much of the year.

The third primitive type was the *Tarpan*. Its natural home was eastern Europe and the southern Russian steppes, and it probably helped give rise to many of our pony and light horse breeds. Engravings said to have been taken from life during the eighteenth and nineteenth centuries show an aggressive-looking, tough, fast, lightweight yet strong pony type. Ponies of Tarpan descent have been gathered together in breeding herds in the vast ancient forests of Poland in an effort to reproduce an animal of as near Tarpan type as is possible now. A viable population now exists.

As the land masses were established into more or less their current configuration, these three primitive types were free to roam and, certainly around the edges of their ranges, would have met and interbred to some extent, melding their types in genetic interchange. Further environmental and climatic changes would have helped evolve these types further. However, it seems that the numbers of horses in general were at a level which would cause alarm in modern-day conservationists – just a few thousand overall had survived down to the time, arguably about five or six thousand years ago, when the horse is first believed to have been properly domesticated, probably by a Ukrainian tribe of hunter-gatherers. It is true that there exist rock paintings and carvings much older than 4000 BC which seem to show horses wearing what look like halters or headcollars, but until firm archaeological evidence arises to prove otherwise, that approximate date is the one most widely accepted as being when horses were first domesticated.

At that time, the three primitive types apparently still existed but also seem to have produced four variants, doubtless aided significantly by the climate and terrain in which they found themselves. This is where some experts disagree but I shall give the most widely accepted version of our domestic horses' forebears. There were two northern pony types with 'cold-blooded' features (see below) and two southern horse types with 'hot-blooded' features.

- *Pony Type 1* lived mainly in north-west Europe and was around 12.1 hands high, strong, nippy, hardy and chunky – and very resistant to wet, wind, cold and privation. It was the type known as the Northern, Celtic or Plateau Pony and probably had large amounts of Tarpan genes. Today it is represented by such types as the Exmoor Pony and the Icelandic Horse.

- *Pony Type 2* was about 14.2 hands high and, living in northern Europe and Asia, was fairly impervious to sub-zero temperatures, poor keep, bitter winds and frost. It would have resembled the Przewalski Horse and had many of its genes. Today, the larger, heavier ponies and cobs such as the Norwegian Fjord and the heavier types of Highland derive from it.

- *Horse Type 3* had evolved as a desert/steppe horse. Around 14.3 hands high, it was spare, lean and 'dry', with great resistance to drought and heat. It lived in central Asia and central and western Europe. It probably had a large dose of Tarpan genes and some from the Przewalski

Horse, but genetic adaptation to a desert environment which developed after the last Ice Age will have forged its desert, 'hot-blood' qualities.

It must have been the closest ancestor of the old Turkmene family of horses and so, today, of the Akhal-Teké, the Turcoman, similar breeds to them and, hence, of the lean, rangy type of Thoroughbred. The Iberian and North African Barb Horses must have generous amounts of its blood and, through them, it has influenced most of the world's breeds, including the trotting breeds and even the more active type of heavy horse, such as the Percheron to name just one.

- *Horse Type 4* was also a desert horse but small at about 12 hands high. Enthusiasts of the Caspian claim it as a direct descendant from this type. Some call it the Proto-Arab (the Arab prototype) and it would have been greatly influenced by the Tarpan as well as by its environment in western Asia. Whereas Horse Type 3 was long and rangy

with perhaps a longish, plain head, Horse Type 4 had a small head with a straight or slightly concave profile and a domed forehead. Its body was short and compact. It was a true wild type and would mate with other types within its reach. It subsequently influenced them and just about every subsequent man-made breed in the world.

These seven main types, then (the three 'originals' and their four descendant types), were probably the raw equine materials from which modern breeds and types, in all their wide diversity of make, shape and inclination, developed. They were what were available to early civilisations who, with all the far-sightedness and enterprise of successful modern business people, undertook the domestication of the horse. The initiative spread and by about 2000 BC horses and ponies were a major part of human society throughout Eurasia: today, at the

The Przewalski Horse exhibits all the characteristics of a natural, cold-climate type of equine, with its large head, short, thick neck, stocky body and camouflage dun colouring

beginning of the twenty-first century AD, the International League for the Protection of Horses (ILPH) estimates that there are about 122 million horses and ponies in the world *of which about 100 million are working animals in developing countries*. This excludes the ubiquitous working donkeys in such countries. Quite a thought.

'Hot-bloods' and 'cold-bloods'

It should be made clear that the expressions 'hot-blooded' and 'cold-blooded' in no way refer to equine blood or body temperature; in a normal, healthy, mature animal, the temperature is 37–38°C or 99–101°F, no matter what breed or type it is. The terms refer not only to the physical but also to the mental characteristics of an animal. Today a very common term, particularly in reference to competition or sports horses, is 'warmblood' which obviously means a blend of the two main types and technically does not apply only to the continental European blend.

Populations of animals which live for many generations in a particular region will only survive there if they develop features which fit them for the prevailing climate and environment. Apart from 'inner' features, relating to the digestive system and the metabolism of food available in a particular area, survival depends very much on ambient temperature – heat or the lack of it. Heat escapes from the body by means

A Shire Horse stallion of around 100 years ago. A breed developed from cold-climate ancestors, its massive proportions and weight belie its activity and action. This old-type of Shire has shorter legs than the modern, longer-legged, taller type of Shire, developed for extra height

of exhalation, sweating, radiation through the skin and convection, being blown away by the wind from the surface of the body.

Cold-blooded features

Horses and ponies which evolved in cold climates are built to retain body heat. The most noticeable features about them are their stocky, chunky, sometimes massive build and their often laid-back temperaments. Cold-bloods such as heavy horses, northern-type ponies and cobs have the following features:

- well-rounded bodies to guard heat in the body core (heat escapes less easily from a barrel than from a radiator)
- thick, short necks (the neck is fairly radiator-shaped so the less there is of it and the thicker it is the better)
- fairly thick skin, which is more difficult for heat to pass through
- long, thick coats of body hair, particularly in winter, and coarse, plentiful mane and tail hair. Hair is hollow and air is a poor conductor of heat; the hair forms, through the overlapping of the individual hairs, an insulating warm air layer next to the skin
- short legs to minimise airflow and, therefore, heat removal, around the body
- proportionately large heads and small, easily closed nostrils, with long nasal passages to warm cold air before it reaches the lungs
- small ears (ears being well supplied with blood) to minimise heat loss from the blood
- low tail carriage to protect the thin-skinned area between the buttocks and on the belly from which heat is easily lost; a behavioural adaptation is to stand with tails to the weather, for this reason
- restricted inclination to sweat as their natural cool to cold environment does not call for it; sweat, being liquid, is an excellent conductor of heat and the production of sweat and its evaporation from the surface of the body carries heat away with it

These physical features all go to make up the familiar 'hairies' many of us find so appealing –

teddy bears in horses' clothing! Many of them, but by no means all, have phlegmatic temperaments and, because of their greater bodyweight for height and comparatively short legs, are not noted for speed or great physical agility such as rapid turning, jumping, sprinting, or (some say) for quick thinking!

Hot-blooded features

Horses and ponies from hot regions look quite different. They are built for easy heat loss, are finer and sometimes have 'hot' or more 'hyper' temperaments. Their particular features include:

- more oval bodies, which means heat from the body core has less distance to travel to the outside
- longer, slimmer necks to further increase the heat-loss area and facility
- thin skin through which heat can pass easily
- coat hair which is often very short, and quite short even in winter, forming much less of a warm air layer to hamper heat loss; the mane and tail hair are often long, fine and silky and much thinner than in cold-bloods so as not to retain heat yet provide limited protection from sun and insects
- proportionately longer legs than cold-bloods, creating more airflow around the body for heat removal
- smaller heads since there is no need for significant warming of inhaled air, and very mobile and open nostrils to enable good air passage – body heat can be easily exhaled with the used air (another reason for the smaller size is said to be because the teeth of hot-bloods are smaller as the vegetation in their natural environment is juicier and easier to chew than in cold regions, so large teeth are unnecessary)
- relatively large ears, as with most desert animals, to facilitate loss of heat from their ample blood supply
- tails which are usually carried well away from their bodies, particularly in motion, again to facilitate airflow and heat removal
- a propensity to sweat very freely to evaporate away excess heat

These features exemplify the typical 'blood' horse, of which there are several breeds and types in the world although most people in the western hemisphere think of Thoroughbreds and Arabs when the terms 'hot-blood' or 'blood horse' are used. The animals are the epitome of what humans call 'breeding', refinement and 'quality' with their thin skin, easily visible blood vessels, long, fine legs and springy gaits, their often proud carriage, their breathtaking speed and athleticism and their alert, sensitive temperaments.

Two more different types of animal within the same species would be hard to imagine, yet they are both *Equus caballus*. From the point of view of the 'jobs' they can each do for man, we generally find that because of their strength and temperamental stability, the larger, heavier cold-bloods are used in draught for heavy or lighter haulage, farm work and jobs in industry, more now in the eastern hemisphere than in the West although by no means exclusively. The lighter, faster hot-bloods and warmbloods are ideal for athletic pursuits such as racing, jumping,

In complete contrast to the photograph on page 16, this top-class Thoroughbred mare is a perfect example of an animal whose ancestors evolved in hot climates, with her thin skin, long, fine legs, long neck and small head

general pleasure riding, smart harness work, competitive riding and driving and stock work, where agility and the ability to think quickly are essential.

Although individual horses can adapt somewhat to changing conditions within their immediate environment, for example by changing their coats with the seasons or 'hardening up' when turned out to live instead of being stabled, these adaptations are limited. A cold-blood can live all its life in a hot climate and still not adapt enough to be suited to it; a hot-blood will never adapt to a winter outdoors on the Shetland Islands or the Russian tundra.

Man has intervened in most horses' lives by artificial selection when breeding (deciding which stallion will mate which mare and, therefore, what features the foal will possess) and in management (hot-bloods, for instance, are only able to live in cold climates because man houses, clothes and feeds them). Thoroughbreds, therefore, thrive in Canada and British native ponies in Arabia and northern Australia because man manipulates their environment, housing and management.

The classic prey animal

Most animals have natural predators. Some are both predator and prey, hunting for food and themselves being hunted, but horses are purely prey animals. Their outlook on life is essentially cautious, and although they may not exactly live on their nerves they are very quick to become wary and startled. Millions of years of watching and listening for danger in the grass has ingrained this feature in the horse.

Apart from being easily alerted, horses are endowed with four essential physical survival features:

- *The ability to get off to a lightning standing start.* This is particularly useful to man in sprint racing, polo, speed jumping, gymkhana games and working cattle, and to the horse in getting a head start on most of its predators provided he senses their presence while they are no less than 7.5 m

(25 ft) away – the horse's approximate 'flight distance'.

- *The ability to reach a top speed of about 70 k.p.h. (45 m.p.h.) in less than four or five seconds.* This is at least as fast as feline predators which are only successful in about one in four chases. Some individuals have been clocked in tests as reaching their top speed in as little as three seconds. This sort of speed is attractive to man for sports and competitions and, formerly, for mounted courier and communication systems.

- *The stamina to maintain reasonable speed over many miles.* This is useful to the horse in defying the wearing-down tactics of canine predators, which are more effective than felines as they make a kill in seven out of ten hunts. Such stamina is obviously of great benefit to man for ridden or driven transport, travel and longer-distance sports such as hunting and the increasingly popular endurance riding.

- *The ability to use minimal energy, to rest and even sleep standing up.* This is due to an adaptation of ligaments and tendons in the legs, known as the 'stay apparatus', which results in the ability to 'lock' the legs at elbow, knee, hock and stifle so that the horse's considerable body weight can be supported without muscular effort. It also means that the horse is already on his feet and ready to flee should danger threaten. Deep sleep has to be experienced lying flat out and is normally limited, particularly in free-living animals subject to predation, because it takes a horse several seconds to get up which could mean the difference between escape and death. This ability to rest standing up is useful to the horse but not fully appreciated by man, who likes horses to 'lie down and rest their legs'.

Other features of the horse which suit it to energy efficiency, speed and agility are:

- *The lack of muscles in the lower legs.* The horse's legs, particularly in the more hot-blooded types, are quite long and light relative to body size; the lack of muscle tissue, which is quite heavy, below knee and hock means that the horse has little weight to move, which makes for energy efficiency and good balance. If the legs were heavy, a

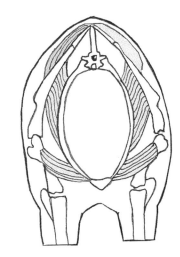

The horse has no shoulder joint as in the human: the thorax and forelimbs are attached solely by various soft tissues, an arrangement known as the 'thoracic sling'

lot of energy would be needed to move them, which would decrease his resources and stamina, and he would find balancing and moving much harder work which, in turn, would hamper his speed and agility. Think of swinging a hammer by its head as opposed to the end of its handle, or a pendulum on a grandfather clock.

As we have seen, the horse's lower legs lengthened during evolution and the number of toes decreased so that the horse is now standing on the equivalent of the end of our middle finger; the joint we call his knee is actually the same as our wrist. The leg is supported in its 'spring-footed' stance by strong, taut tendons and ligaments (see Chapter 3) which assist this economical movement.

- *Relatively small, light feet on the ends of the limbs.* Again, this lack of a heavy weight on the ends of the legs makes for energy efficiency. One has to draw a fine line with the weight of a horse's shoes: racehorses wear very light (usually aluminium) shoes called racing plates to reduce weight and assist speed, whereas draught horses, particularly 'heavies', usually wear heavy ones for extra wear. However, shoes that are too heavy come down that much harder and so wear that much more quickly; they also subject the feet and legs to more concussion.

- *The 'thoracic sling'.* The horse's ribcage is supported between the shoulder blades and humerus or upper arm bone by muscle tissue, tendons, ligaments and connective tissue or fascia: there is no collar bone and no shoulder joint as in humans. This arrangement greatly helps reduce concussion during fast gaits as the soft tissues absorb a great deal of it.

The ideal partner

All these physical features of the horse fit him ideally as an efficient prey animal often well able to escape predation by his natural enemies. It is incidental and very convenient for us that they also enable him to do various jobs for us according to his natural type. He is comfortable to sit on and even though his back was certainly not designed to carry weight it can do so safely for him and us *if* he is correctly ridden, and worked gymnastically to build up his strength. He is fast, which is exhilarating for us in sports (ridden and driven). He has stamina, which has made him a viable proposition for transport, trade, war, communication and so on. He is strong in both weight-carrying and traction. Finally, he is a herd-orientated, social animal, not naturally aggressive, and enjoys the company of those creatures he likes and trusts. This means that although most horses are happiest when with their own kind they can and do form strong bonds and rewarding relationships with humans. It is much more pleasant and effective to work, and play, with a co-operative partner.

CHAPTER

2

DOMESTICATION AND SPECIALISATION

Exactly what the first steps were in domesticating the horse will probably never be known. It is fairly certain, though, that man first saw the horse as food on the hoof and hunted it as he would any other animal he thought he could catch or kill. Learning how best to capture or corner horses led by means of life-dependent observation to a naturally acquired knowledge of equine behaviour. Different tactics would be employed, such as driving herds over cliffs and into blind gulleys, building fenced-in areas into which herds were driven and individuals cornered, captured with ropes and butchered. Hunting on the run and killing horses with spears and, later, bows and arrows, were doubtless also found to be effective and, during this process, the hunters could not fail to develop a first-hand appreciation of the speed, stamina and, once caught, sheer physical strength of the horse – all far superior to the bovine species which were already domesticated and worked.

Early man – and the very few remaining non-farming peoples today – followed wild herds and their own animals as they followed their natural intuition to find new grazing grounds. Feral herds still do this today, of course; when one area is grazed down they migrate to another, perhaps nearby or maybe many miles away. Different species of grazing animals feed together, each being adapted to eat different grasses or even different parts of grasses. For example, zebra, antelope and wildebeest are constant grazing partners in Africa, where the

wildebeest and antelope eat the heads of the grasses and the softer leafy parts whereas the zebras prefer the tougher, more fibrous stalks.

The horses would be hunted mainly for meat but their hide, hair, bones, horn and teeth would also be used for tools, clothing, tents, household and personal items, weapons and jewellery. The first horses actually to be captured and kept would have been those that were easier to catch and handle such as young animals, injured, sick or older ones, and heavily pregnant or freshly foaled mares. These would have been tethered or corralled and may well have attracted others. Capturing heavily pregnant or newly foaled mares would have been an ideal way to start to build up a herd. The practice of tethering a captive in-season mare near the edges of an encampment so that a wild or feral stallion would come and cover her has continued into living memory and still happens in some countries. All these ruses would eventually result in tribes building up their own herds of horses. The use of horse milk and blood as food for humans and other animals would have followed quickly once the horses were prisoners, and those born in captivity would come to accept man as part of their lives and remain as a matter of course, as horses do today on the Asian steppes, near the tribal or family encampment, maybe with human 'minders' on horseback.

The first thought of using horses for work may have been incidental although, as cattle were already used for draught, the use of horses, with their superior physical qualities if more challenging temperament and behaviour, may have followed naturally. Once some horses were cornered and fenced in, milling around in terror, it is not inconceivable that some of the more agile, braver members of the human tribe might have used the backs of some horses as 'stepping stones' to reach others in order to separate them from the herd, and so riding may have been born.

Whether riding or driving came first is still argued about among equestrian historians but I feel that pack work probably came before either. Maybe, as the family and herd migrated to fresh feeding grounds, a human walking alongside a tame, amenable horse and carrying a heavy burden, would rest it on the horse's back for temporary relief. Then it would be realised that some form of retaining harness, pad or container, such as a pannier, would ensure that the horse carried this burden for longer. This could have led to traces for pulling a travois for larger loads and sick or injured people. Old people, very young ones or injured ones, not to mention pregnant women, may also have been hoisted onto horses' backs for transport and have become the first passenger-riders. The development of sleds and ultimately wheeled vehicles would follow but in exactly what order we shall probably never know.

What is certain is that these early tribes and civilisations would have been quick to realise that certain body shapes and physical abilities were suitable for different requirements – a broad back and strong build was ideal not only for meat to eat but also for heavy pack and draught work or carrying incapacitated humans, while a lighter, faster build was suited for carrying messengers quickly to neighbouring tribes or to scout the lie of the land ahead and report back in time to avoid trouble. Hunting from horseback would make that vital task so much easier and the horses could also be used to carry or drag home the catch.

Other equines apart from horses have been domesticated over the ages but only the donkey, a descendant of the African wild ass of the Bible has proved lastingly successful. The Babylonians and Assyrians are famous for having temporarily used onagers for work but their grossly uncooperative temperament must have made life pretty unpleasant for their handlers and the enterprise was abandoned. Zebras have certainly been domesticated and used for riding and draught but only the horse has remained permanently and increasingly popular as man's slave, friend and work- and playmate.

The horse for the job

Because of the widely differing jobs for which man used the horse, it became obvious that different types and builds were better suited to each task. Although early peoples would have had access only to the equidae indigenous to their own region, as the horse made travel and trade easier and more feasible they would come across different types of horses from those with which they were familiar.

Horses have long been used as both merchandise and currency. There was, for example, a tremendous trade in China's Heavenly Horses; Persian Arabs, still among the most desired equines in the Eastern world, were very much in demand and one horse was worth two camels in ancient Arabia and could be exchanged for ten cows in Persia. And once domesticated horses became widespread across Eurasia, the original wild types and their immediate descendants described in Chapter 1 would soon all enter an Old World melting pot.

War has always been accompanied and followed by looting and horses were a favourite booty right up to and including the Second World War. Many of today's competition warmbloods are based immediately on native stock which 'changed hands' during the two world wars. Napoleon and his soldiers were noted for stealing their vanquished enemies' horses all over Europe, accepting them as bribes or exchanging them for imprisoned VIPs. The Crusaders brought back from the Orient the 'new', fast sports cars of the day – the horses we now call Arabs, and also Barbs and Turks. Before them the Romans filched, stole, bought and bartered horseflesh of every sort, from orientals for chariot racing and officers' chargers to eastern European heavy horses for haulage. Even earlier peoples than they traditionally exchanged horses of every sort, shape and size in various ways. It now seems clear, for example, that fine oriental horses were imported into what became Britain by peoples far more sophisticated than we have until now imagined, many centuries before the Romans brought their own eastern chargers.

Man's perception and intelligence fairly soon turned him into an expert breeder of animals and the passing on of different physical and psychological qualities from parents to offspring would be closely noted. People were no different then from now in wanting what was different, foreign and hard to obtain, preferably before anyone else had it, and they would readily breed from acquired animals to create just the sort of horse they were looking for by passing on qualities absent from their own stock.

Although horses are used mainly for leisure purposes, in the western hemisphere at any rate, our pleasure is still their work and they remain athletic animals required mainly for work today rather than for human food – although this is usually their final service to man in some countries in continental Europe. Some of the heavier breeds are produced there, and in Japan and other Eastern countries, mainly for meat. It is no miracle that we have not ended up with one ubiquitous horse – a horse for all reasons. It says much for early man's immediate perception of horseflesh that different breeds (although not perhaps in the sense in which we use the term today) and specific types were soon developed according to the purpose for which they were wanted. From the original seven natural types which existed after the end of the last Ice Age there are now hundreds of different breeds and types of horse and pony all over the world, all 'man-made'. The continents of America and Australasia, which had no indigenous horses of their own (although the horse species originated in America and died out there around the end of the last Ice Age), are among the most enthusiastic regions of the world when it comes to the use

and breeding of horses, and they are still creating their own breeds for specific and sometimes quite narrowly defined purposes, particularly the U.S.A.

Over the past several thousand years, then, man has used and created horses and ponies for many different jobs according to physique and temperament. These jobs include: pack work; draught, from heavy transport to light, fast and elegant carriages, not to mention chariot racing and modern trotting/harness racing; stock work; courier and light transport services; coaching in its heyday; and sport from polo (the oldest) to ridden racing, mainly at the gallop but also ridden trotting races which are especially popular in France, and all manner of equestrian sports involving jumping – something which, contrary to popular opinion, many horses do naturally, are good at and often enjoy.

Without the services of heavy draught horses with their massive build and amenable natures, civilisations could not have developed and flourished; without warhorses of every conceivable type from lightweight orientals to the stocky cobs which carried the knights and the heavy horses which pulled artillery and the regiment's supplies, empires could not have been built and conquered; without the fast, smart roadsters or trotters, trade and communication would have been so much more difficult; and without the creation of the elegant, temperamental, spirited and low-slung Thoroughbred, the world would have been denied its most famous breed and, to many sensitive and competent horsemen and women, the only breed they care to ride. For, like many other breeds and types, the Thoroughbred is versatile: racing is far from its only job.

It must be stressed that any well-conformed horse can do virtually any job, within reason, but there are certain conformational features and temperamental qualities that make some better fitted to certain roles than others. Moreover, our modern knowledge of muscle type and function enables us more easily to select 'the horse for the job'. Muscles can contract or 'twitch' fast or slowly; some can work well with little or no oxygen and are suitable, for example, for fast work such as sprinting in which oxygen cannot be supplied fast enough to meet the muscles' requirements, but others can only work with an ample oxygen supply and are suited to medium- to long-term work performed at a slower pace, such as hunting or endurance riding, for instance, in which the body can easily supply oxygen at the rate at which the muscles demand it. These factors, as much as actual conformation, determine our choice of the right horse for the job, and they are discussed in Chapter 3.

We are not there yet

Man has been breeding horses for particular purposes for thousands of years and one would have thought that we should have a fairly foolproof system by now, by which we can mate Stallion A with Mare B and know for certain what qualities their foal is going to inherit. But we do not. We can form a good idea but despite our modern knowledge of DNA 'fingerprinting' and genetics, we still cannot be *certain* what genes a foal will inherit. Even full siblings from

Miss Sylvia Stanier, LVO, long-reins her Oldenburg stallion, the late Adel, in a High School display, here caught by the camera just before flying change. The Oldenburg is a perfect example of a continental warmblood breed, definitely bred for a purpose – modern competitive disciplines, particularly dressage and showjumping. (Photo: Peter Sweet)

the same stallion and mare year after year cannot be guaranteed to be very alike because of the random way in which genes are inherited at mating.

The old saying 'mate the best to the best and hope for the best' is still followed by most practical breeders but those who are more 'on-the-ball' make a study of which genes appear to be dominant in a particular mare and stallion and, therefore, which characteristics are repeatedly expressed in their offspring. The breeding of American Standardbreds and continental European warmbloods, to give just two examples, has been refined to such an extent by astute, perceptive and knowledgeable breeders that they can be fairly sure what a foal from a particular mating will look like, what its conformation is likely to be and what job it is likely to be suitable for. In the case of the Standardbreds, which are bred for trotting and pacing races in harness, even the foal's likely speed can be estimated with reasonable accuracy, down to the nearest second or two. The warmbloods, too,

have specific 'lines', such as dressage lines or showjumping lines (warmbloods' two best *métiers*), and will know what talents a foal from a given mating is likely to have.

The British and Irish are less precision-minded on the whole and still trust a good deal to luck. There are a few exceptions who can be relied on *consistently* to produce horses suited to particular jobs – the Welton Stud of event horses is just one example. Our event horses, for example, are still among the best in the world although, at the time of writing, New Zealand is repeatedly producing major international Thoroughbred winners in this discipline. There are those who feel that breeding would be deadly boring if breeders knew exactly what sort of foal was going to be produced from any particular mating – the uncertainty is half the fun, but not when breeding is your living. In any case, the whole situation is still uncertain enough to ensure that horses of moderate to appalling conformation will still be produced well into the unforeseeable future!

CHAPTER

3

THE SKELETON AND HOW IT MOVES

The horse's skeleton is often described as the 'scaffolding' around which the body is built. Like a lot of horsey jargon, this is not strictly accurate; scaffolding is relatively rigid and cannot move – if it does the results can be disastrous. The skeleton, on the other hand, is specifically meant to move, often very fast and athletically. It is a moveable framework of bone and cartilage (gristle) formed into a system of joints, levers, fulcrums and so on which is held together by ligaments and made to move by the action of muscles pulling on tendons, this movement being controlled by the nervous system. *It is the form and proportions of the skeleton which determine a horse or pony's true conformation – nothing else.*

The skeleton is covered by muscles, tendons, fat, connective tissue (a fibrous and varied type of body tissue), and other soft tissues such as blood and lymphatic vessels, skin and hair. But nothing we do to the muscles in particular by means of work, aimed at developing them in chosen ways to enhance a horse's appearance or capabilities, will change his basic conformation, although faults can certainly be disguised and function improved by appropriate work and resultant muscular development.

Foals born with conformational faults, particularly in the feet and legs, can often be helped a good deal by vets and farriers through surgery and other techniques, or corrective trimming and shoeing. Bones and feet can be 'trained' into a more normal form but this has to be done very

early in life. After the age of six months (some say earlier) the bones are too hardened and mature to be changed at all easily.

The bone structure of mature animals with significant conformation faults cannot be improved and their management and training can only ameliorate these faults to some degree by means of correct gymnastic work and muscular development. Conversely, faulty training, poor riding or driving techniques (including badly fitting or adjusted tack and harness) and poor farriery can all change a horse's body, appearance and action for the worse and actually cause injury. A well-conformed horse can be made to look positively deformed and it takes a skilled eye to see through the mismanagement to the physical qualities beneath. Once the root cause is corrected, it is amazing what an improvement can be made to a horse's appearance, to his apparent conformation and to his action.

A case in point is a ewe neck, which usually goes with a poorly developed 'topline' along the back, loins and quarters. Although this is a conformational fault of the neck vertebrae and the set-on of the head, with which a horse is born, correct, sensitive riding and ground work can improve it (and, in fact, develop and educate any horse) basically by encouraging the horse to do the following things, ideally on long reins or, failing that, on the lunge, so that he does not have to counteract the weight of a rider:

a) A ewe or upside-down neck causes a horses usually to resist the bit and to go naturally with his back sagging and hind legs trailing. Correct work helps greatly to improve matters, however

b) A standing martingale is often fitted to ewe-necked horses in the mistaken belief that, by forcibly keeping the head down, the horse will develop correct musculature and be improved. What actually happens is that the force exerted by the horse's pushing his head up and out is blocked by the noseband; this creates tension in the neck muscles and often simply causes him to kink his neck downwards just in front of the withers in an effort to escape the discomfort. It, therefore, does not solve the problem at all

- Engage his hindquarters, lowering them and bringing his hindlegs further forward under his belly.
- Work with the neck lowered (forward and down), flexing or 'giving' at the poll as well as his conformation allows so that he is working in the familiar 'long-and-low' posture but never so that the front line of his face comes behind a line vertical to the ground with the chin drawn towards the chest (known popularly as 'overbent' and 'working deep'), which, as a teacher of classical riding, I believe to be physically and psychologically disadvantageous.
- Raise his back, which will be partly a natural result of lowering the quarters and head (unless the horse has an injury or a bad rider) and partly due to his use of his belly muscles, and others, to raise the spine from below.

These techniques are correct, basic training for all horses although many never receive the benefits of them. Correctly performed, and not overdone (say twenty minutes a day five days a week), they can do a very great deal to enhance any horse's apparent conformation and general muscular development (along with other specific exercises). This work allows the muscles along the topline of the horse's neck, back, loins and quarters to function beneficially, alternately slightly contracting and being stretched, allowing an ample flow of blood and lymph through them resulting in healthy development, neither 'stringy' and flat nor hypertrophied and 'muscle-bound'. Our ewe-necked horse will look a great deal better – but it will still be ewe-necked!

Functions of the skeleton

The skeleton gives shape and support to the body; without it, the remaining parts would be so much floppy tissue on the ground.

The hard bone in its various formats also protects the sensitive, softer structures and organs. The skull protects the brain and the vertebrae (individual bones of the spine or backbone) protect the spinal cord which is an extension of the brain and runs through the internal tunnel they form. The ribcage protects the heart and lungs, the pelvis, the lumbar or loin area and the sacrum or croup area of the spine protect the reproductive organs, the urinary organs and the hind end of the intestinal tract.

Because of its structure, with bones as levers, joints, supportive ligaments and 'movers' like muscles and tendons, the skeleton enables the body to move. Moreover, bone stores the minerals calcium, phosphorus and magnesium which can be held or withdrawn as the body requires. It is also the place where blood cells are made and, to some extent, stored.

Living bone

Bone is far from being the hard, rigid, insensitive tissue that many people think it is. It is made of living cells and consists of protein and minerals.

It grows variously from its ends, from its sides and from inside. As we have seen, blood cells are made inside bones, and they are also used by the body as a reservoir of calcium, phosphorus and magnesium. Bone is well supplied with blood and lymph vessels (lymph being a supportive fluid to blood), and also with nerves, and is able to heal itself if it is diseased or injured; indeed bone heals better than any other body tissue, although sometimes the actual form of the injury or disease makes euthanasia necessary. A badly shattered leg, for instance, usually means the horse has to be put down but cleaner breaks can nowadays often be repaired to allow healing to take place. Many horses have in the past been put down due to navicular disease but it is now believed that this condition is mainly one of inappropriate foot trimming, which causes too much pressure on the navicular bone from the tendon running over it inside the foot; suitable trimming and shoeing, along with medication, can now greatly help this condition.

Bone can grow and 'shrink' (known as remodelling), according to the demands and stresses placed on it by physical exertion and, conversely, it can also deteriorate with lack of exercise. This is only one good reason for ensuring that horses constantly receive plenty of exercise. Horses who live wild have natural, reasonably constant stresses on their skeletons whereas the demands on the bones of domestic, working horses are much more unnatural and erratic, resulting in problems. The common lifestyle of athletically working horses in the Western world, for instance, involves the horse being stabled for most of his time with occasional spurts of activity or actual hard work. This is far from beneficial for the bone because the enforced inactivity (averaging twenty-two hours out of twenty-four!) causes it to deteriorate and weaken and the skeleton as a moving machine to stiffen. Subsequent periods of around two hours a day of exercise and perhaps harder work suddenly stress the structure, which is now not well placed to withstand this stress, and injuries occur such as concussion to bones and joints, tiny fractures which may go unrecognised, splints, bone spavins, ringbone, navicular disease and other forms of osteoarthritis, worn cartilage and also 'sprained' tendons and ligaments and 'torn' muscles. Sometimes these injuries are tiny but repeated and result in a generally uncomfortable, slightly painful body, which adversely affects the horse's way of going and willingness to work.

If the horse lived a more natural lifestyle, his skeleton would be stronger and able to withstand the stresses of the work we ask him to do. This is not impossible with sensible housing, management and feeding but traditional methods and ideas die hard, even when the advantages of change are clear.

Types of bone

There are two main types of bone, plus cartilage. The first is *dense*, *compact*, or *cortical* bone, such as the hard bone which forms the outer cylinder or shaft of the long leg bones. Then there is *spongy* or *cancellous* bone, which is composed of thin, intersecting leaves and is found at the ends of the long bones and inside short bones. It also lines the cavity of dense bone where it is filled with marrow.

Cartilage is a gristly type of bone, again of various types. It is rubbery and fibrous in texture, and made of protein and carbohydrate. Young horses' skeletons contain more cartilage than those of older horses. It acts as a buffer at the ends of bones and is an important part of the skeleton's growth and development mechanism, as cartilage is one of the media of bone formation: bone forms within cartilage which gradually gives way to the proliferating bone cells as the horse matures. This process is best known to horse people as the one which takes place in the 'growth plates' or epiphyses at the ends of the long leg bones when youngsters are growing. An unbalanced diet can disrupt the growth process and cause leg deformities; youngsters' legs can also be injured in this area due to excessive work. Very generally, horses mature from the ground up and the feet and leg bones are the first to develop, doing so by the time the horse is roughly two years old.

Many people do not realise that the spine is the final part to mature and that many horses' spines are not fully developed until five, six or even seven years old, depending on breed and type as well as growth and development rates. Horses' backs – their component vertebrae, joints and associated soft tissues – come in for a great deal of stress when they work, whether ridden or driven, because as well as possibly carrying about a sixth of the horse's own weight, the spine transmits the force or energy from the hindlegs which push the horse forwards. Back problems – injuries to both bone and soft tissues – are much more common in horses than people generally appreciate and are a major cause of poor performance and 'difficult' behaviour in my experience as a teacher, trainer and therapist.

Structure of the skeleton

The skeleton is considered, for convenience, as having two parts:

- the axial skeleton which comprises the skull, the spine or backbone, the ribs and the sternum or breastbone, together called the torso
- the appendicular skeleton which comprises the limbs; the scapulae or shoulder blades are included as part of the forelimbs and the pelvis as part of the hindlimbs.

The horse has no clavicle or collar bone and the forelimb is attached to the thorax/ribcage by muscles, tendons and ligaments; therefore, there is no bony attachment (such as our own shoulder joint) between the forelimb (part of the appendicular skeleton) and the axial skeleton.

The hindlimb, however, is attached to the pelvis by the ball-and-socket hip joint, and the pelvis itself (a 'ring' of fused bones) attaches towards the front and top part of the triangular-shaped sacrum (part of the spine) by means of the left and right sacro-iliac joints. (The ilia or 'wings' of the pelvis – which we commonly call the points of the hips – join to the sacrum, hence the name of these joints.)

Bones

There are about 210 bones in the horse's skeleton, each obviously associated with one or more joints. Bones are named and classified according to their shape.

- *Long bones* (those of the legs) are the largest in the body and are roughly tubular in shape. Their centre parts or shafts are called the diaphyses and their ends the epiphyses. They work as levers during movement and also as supports.
- *Short (cuboid) bones* are found in the knee and hock where there are several in rows. They absorb concussion and contain spongy bone.
- *Sesamoid bones* act as pulleys over which tendons run to facilitate movement and reduce friction, so they are closely involved with muscles and their tendons. The patella or kneecap, the navicular bones in the feet, the fetlock sesamoids and the pisiform bone of the knee are examples.
- *Flat bones* are those in the skull and shoulder blade. They are quite thin and are protective (the skull protects the brain and is made up of thirty-seven bones joined, or rather fused, together), and also provide an attachment for muscles (the scapula or shoulder blade receives some of the powerful forehand muscles).
- *Pneumatic bones* are hollow, containing sinuses or air spaces, such as those of the skull.

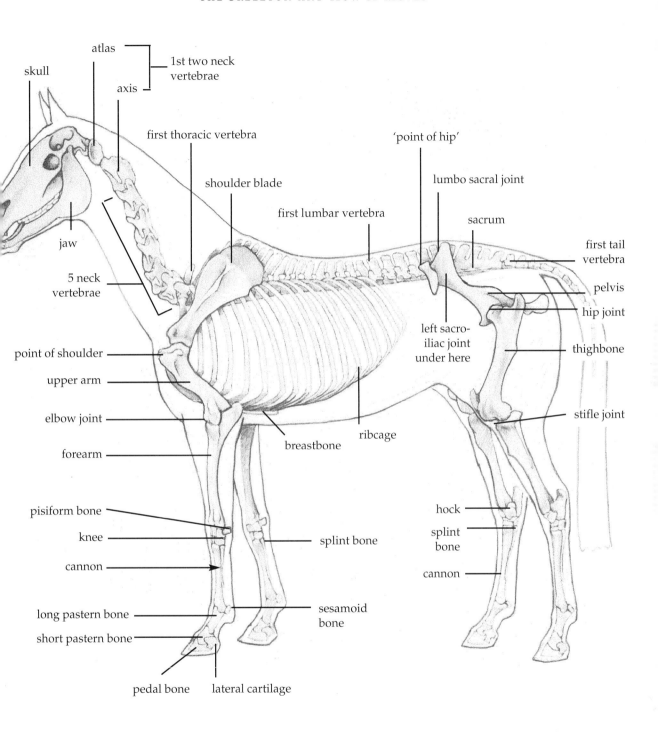

skull

atlas

1st two neck
vertebrae

axis

first thoracic vertebra

'point of hip'

lumbo sacral joint

shoulder blade

first lumbar vertebra

sacrum

jaw

first tail
vertebra

5 neck
vertebrae

pelvis

hip joint

left sacro-
iliac joint
under here

thighbone

point of shoulder

upper arm

stifle joint

elbow joint

ribcage

forearm

breastbone

pisiform bone

hock

splint
bone

knee

splint bone

cannon

cannon

long pastern bone

short pastern bone

sesamoid
bone

pedal bone   lateral cartilage

Parts of the skeleton

- *Irregular bones* are those of the spine – the vertebrae – which are of very varied shape and size. They have large or small projections or processes as points of muscle attachment and run the entire length of the horse from the poll to the tip of the tail.

There are seven cervical or neck vertebrae, eighteen thoracic (chest and upper back) vertebrae, six lumbar (loin area) vertebrae, five fused or joined sacral (pelvic/croup) vertebrae and fifteen to twenty caudal or coccygeal (tail) vertebrae.

Attached mainly by cartilage to the transverse (side) processes of the vertebrae are the ribs – eight pairs of true ribs, so called because they are directly attached to the breastbone underneath the chest, and ten pairs of false ribs, which are connected at their ends to each other, again by cartilage, and so indirectly to the last pair of true ribs and thence to the breastbone, the whole forming the ribcage. This is quite a flexible structure, enabling the lungs to expand greatly and relax again during athletic work.

Each vertebra (except the lower tail vertebrae) has a hole in its middle so that, placed end to end as they are, they form a tunnel down which runs the spinal cord (an extension of the brain and a vital part of the nervous system), which itself sends out branching nerves through matched-up grooves at the joints between the vertebrae.

Joints

There are three types of joint in the skeleton. *Moveable joints* are those with which we are most familiar. The basic design consists of two articulating, cartilage-covered bone ends surrounded by a joint sac or bursa. There is an inner membranous lining which produces lubricating synovia or joint oil and an outer sac or membrane; bands of ligament also surround the joint to support and bind it together. Bursae are found at sites where there is significant pressure. There are different kinds of moveable joints:

- hinge joints which permit movement largely in one direction or plane, like the elbow and fetlock

joints – although these can be rotated very slightly (and gently) by trained people during physical therapies
- the ball-and-socket joint at the hip, where the 'ball' at the top of the thigh bone or femur fits into a socket in the pelvis; it is the only one of this kind in the horse, and permits movement in three planes – forward–backward movement, restricted inward movement under the body (adduction) and, in the horse, only very slight outward movement away from the body (abduction)
- pivot joints, which are the one between the skull and the first cervical or neck vertebra, the atlas, which permits the horse to nod his head, and the one between the atlas and the second cervical vertebra, the axis, which permits the horse to rotate his head to some extent and move it from side to side
- gliding joints such as those in the knee (equivalent to our wrist) and hock (equivalent to our ankle), where the several cuboid bones glide over one another, and also the stifle joint (the patella or knee cap equivalent to our knee)

Slightly moveable joints are those like the ones between the vertebrae (although there is still argument among equestrians over whether the spine is really flexible or not). There is cushioning cartilage between the vertebrae for protection and the spine as a whole certainly is slightly flexible. The common analogy of a 'chain' of vertebrae forming the spine is, however and rather obviously, quite incorrect because the vertebrae articulate against one another at these slightly moveable joints: they are not linked through each other like a chain.

Another slightly moveable joint, or rather pair of joints, are the left and right sacro-iliac joints which tightly join the ilia or wings of the pelvis to the sacrum by means of cartilage, ligaments and synovial (sac) structures. The attachment has casually been referred to as a 'velcro-like' fastening (tight and close) which allows very limited movement.

Fixed joints are joins, rather than joints, between bones where the latter have fused together during evolution. There is still a thin layer of connective tissue or cartilage between them. The bones of the skull and pelvis are examples. The croup of the horse (the sacrum which continues on behind the lumbar or loin area) is another, being formed of five fused vertebrae the first of which articulates with the last of the lumbar vertebrae at the lumbo-sacral joint.

The location of this joint in the horse can be felt as a soft little dip in the spine just in front of the point of the croup (its highest part) and it is this system which is crucial to the performance of both horse and rider. In the rider, it is the main joint which someone riding correctly and well will flex to absorb or 'go with' the movements of the horse's body and so avoid thumping him in the back with the seatbones, particularly in sitting trot and canter (movements which, through incorrect riding, apparently cause so much back soreness in dressage horses at all levels). In the horse, it is the lumbo-sacral joint which largely enables the horse to engage his hindquarters (tuck his bottom under) which, in turn, tilts the back lower part of the pelvis downwards and forwards, and also therefore the hip joints and thigh bones, bringing the hindlegs further forward under the body and creating the flexion of the hindleg joints which is needed for efficient, powerful thrust with minimal danger to the back in particular. This subject is discussed in Chapter 4.

Ligaments

Ligaments are made of strong, fibrous tissue which connects bones or cartilages. They support and strengthen joints and, therefore, the entire skeleton. They can be long, like those running down the neck and back or short like those between vertebrae, simple cord shapes like those in the lower legs or complicated like the nuchal ligament which runs down the crest of the neck and then fans out in sections to attach to the cervical or neck vertebrae below. They can also be bands or sheets of tissue, wrapped around and helping to secure joints or support organs.

The 'stay apparatus' of the horse relies mainly on ligaments but also on many other muscles and tendons. This apparatus is found in all four limbs and enables the horse to stand with little or no muscular effort, and therefore expenditure of energy, by 'locking' the legs so that he can sleep and rest standing up. It also helps prevent over-extension of lower leg joints and reduces concussion during movement.

In this apparatus, there is an exception to the normal rule of ligaments attaching bone to bone or cartilage. In the legs, the short check ligaments attach bone to tendon to take some of the strain and save muscular effort. In the foreleg a check ligament goes from the radius (forearm bone) to the superficial flexor tendon and from the knee to the deep digital flexor tendon. In the hindleg, the tarsal check ligament goes from the tarsus or hock joint to the deep digital flexor tendon below it. This system, only partly detailed here, allows the check ligaments to take the strain from the tendons, obviating effort by their muscles and allowing the tendons to operate as ligaments.

Because the horse carries most weight on the forehand when standing resting, the tarsal check ligaments are thinner than those in the forelegs. (The horse at rest carries about two-thirds of his weight on his forelegs and one-third on his hindlegs, or sometimes on only one hindleg when he is resting its partner, as he often will when resting or sleeping standing up.)

Ligament tissue is only very slightly elastic and is poorly supplied with blood. Hence, ligament injuries are fairly common in athletic horses and can take months or years to recover, and then never to the original state of the tissue. Injuries can be traumatic as in a single major over-extension or insupportable stress or, more commonly, due to repeated tiny injuries which ultimately make the tissue weaker than normal and susceptible to injury it would normally be able to withstand. From a conformation viewpoint, in horses who are poorly made and move badly, the ligaments will take more strain than in well-made, good movers and will, therefore, suffer more injuries. Good conformation makes for sounder horses!

Muscles and tendons

These are considered together because they are really one unit, tendons running from their associated muscles and being a modified form of muscle tissue.

There are three types of muscle tissue:

- *Smooth, visceral or involuntary muscle.* The working of this type is automatic and outside the control of the horse. It is found in such places as the walls of the intestines where it pushes food along, the wall of the uterus where it is responsible for contractions during birth, the arteries and the bladder.
- *Cardiac muscle.* This is very specialised and found only in the walls of the heart. It is responsible for its beating and also works automatically (but is not described as involuntary). It never tires and is independent in that, if conditions are right, it can keep the heart beating even when it is taken from the body.
- *Skeletal muscle* This is mainly under the control of the horse and so is also called *voluntary* muscle. This is the type which 'clothes' the body and moves the bones, and it is the only type in which we are interested in relation to conformation and action. Its purposes are to move the horse's body and to help it keep its balance.

Skeletal muscles make up over a third of the horse's bodyweight – more in a fit, muscled-up horse – and as muscle tissue or meat weighs more than fat, being about 60 per cent water, this is the reason horses tend to slim down (lose fat) but increase in bodyweight as they become fitter and muscled-up. However, horses with a fair covering of fat, which is a poor conductor of heat and so acts as insulation, are more resistant to cold weather while fit, muscular ones have little or no spare fat and tend to feel the cold, depending on their type and taking into account that they are usually clipped, if in work. Thin horses with little muscle or fat may have a long winter coat but will still feel the cold even when wearing a rug, although it will help to protect them.

There are over 700 skeletal muscles in the horse. Each has a *point of origin* where it attaches to a stable (non-moving) bone in the skeleton, running into a fleshy 'belly' portion and ending at an *insertion (or attachment) point* on the bone it

is intended to move. The belly part will pass over at least one joint. Muscles which have an insertion point some way from the belly, such as those of the upper legs which have insertion points around the pasterns and feet, have an

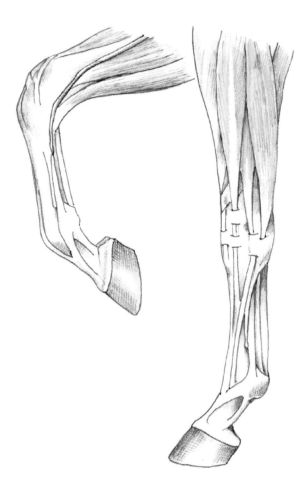

Diagram of the muscles and tendons of the forelegs. There are no muscles below the knee (or the hock in the hindleg) and the feet are relatively small for such a big animal: this makes for economic use of energy as the furthest point from the source of movement (the muscles) is thus very light and easy to move fast. As the muscles behind the forearm contract (as in the right leg), they shorten and exert a pull on their tendons behind the cannon attached to the leg and foot below, which forces the leg to rise and flex. To straighten out the leg, the muscles at the front of the forearm pull similarly on their tendons, which straightens out the leg again. When the leg is stationary on the ground (left leg), opposing muscle groups in the leg, plus associated tendons and ligaments, hold it in balanced tension

extension of modified muscle tissue called a tendon which inserts onto the bones to be moved.

Muscle tissue is capable of contracting or shortening, and so of exerting a force or pull on the insertion point on one bone, forcing it to move, via the joint, closer to the origin on another. This is how movement occurs. Muscles which bend a joint are called *flexors* and those which reverse this action and straighten a joint are called *extensors*. Those which cause a limb to move outwards away from the body are called *abductors* and those which cause it to move inwards under the body are called *adductors*.

Muscles are sensitive, responding to chemical and electrical stimuli via the nervous system. They are able to conduct or pass on stimuli, they are able to contract, as mentioned, and are also very elastic. They work (cause movement) by contracting and can be stretched by the action of opposing muscles. They often work in groups, and have opposing partners which not only stretch them but also limit their actions and 'balance each other out', so helping to prevent such injuries as over-extension of joints and overstretched muscles, tendons and ligaments. They are often in a state of complementary *tonus*, which not only means that they are ready for work at all times but that they are able to help a standing horse keep his balance by small counteracting contractions, even when his stay apparatus is not in operation.

Muscle tissue is made largely of protein; its cells are long fibres arranged in bundles held together by a membrane, each fibre being composed of smaller myofibrils ('myo' means related to muscle) also arranged in bundles within each fibre. It is the action of these fibres and fibrils, which contract by sliding over each other, that causes the muscle to contract and thicken. The horse is born with a set number of fibres which cannot be increased. They can, however, be made larger in response to stress (work) and with suitable servicing by the circulatory system – in other words, by means of adequate supplies, delivered by the blood, of oxygen and nutrients and removal by the blood of the main waste product of energy consumption or work, which

is carbon dioxide. The alternate contraction and relaxation of the muscles squeezes the tiny blood vessels (capillaries) within them so that blood is pushed out, to be replaced by a fresh supply.

There are two main types of muscle fibre which help determine what tasks a horse is best suited for. *Slow-twitch fibres* twitch or move relatively slowly and need a ready supply of oxygen; they are suitable for such work as hunting, endurance riding, eventing, steeplechasing, dressage, trekking/hacking and so on.

Fast-twitch fibres are of two types: high oxidative and low-oxidative. High-oxidative fibres move or twitch faster and use oxygen, so they are good for fairly fast work over long periods of time such as hunting in a galloping country, relatively short but fast-paced endurance riding, active hacking, long- and middle-distance racing and so on. Low-oxidative fibres work the most rapidly and powerfully using little or no oxygen and are used for sprinting, jumping against the clock, polo, cattle-cutting and the like. However, such anaerobic (without oxygen) work produces not only carbon dioxide but the toxin lactic acid, which makes the environment in the muscle too acid and is responsible for the ache and pain of overworked muscles and the onset of fatigue. Therefore, horses with a high predominance of low-oxidative fast-twitch fibres can only work at peak performance for fairly short periods (a horse cannot gallop flat out for several miles, only for a few furlongs).

Most muscles contain some of all types of fibre: it is the amounts of each which dictate the sort of work to which a horse is suited. A simple and painless procedure called a muscle biopsy can be carried out in which a tiny sample of living muscle tissue is removed from the horse and examined under a microscope to see what type of fibre predominates. However, very few owners have this done; most wait to see how the horse performs. The horse can, quite unconsciously and naturally, use, or recruit as it is called, whatever types of fibre he needs for what he happens to be doing – anything from leaping out of a starting gate to wandering slowly over to a new patch of grass.

The types of jobs horses can best do may also be guessed fairly accurately not only from their type, make and shape but also from their muscular development. Horses such as puissance jumpers, cutting horses and sprinters normally have chunky, powerful muscles, whereas staying racehorses, carriage horses and endurance horses have long, lean muscles.

The fastest breed of horse in the world over very short distances (1/4 mile) is the American Quarter Horse, which has a high preponderance of low-oxidative fast-twitch fibres as well as a famously chunky muscular development, particularly in the hindquarters. Endurance horses, staying racehorses and steeplechasers, however, have more slow-twitch fibres than anything else, as well as longer, leaner muscles. Have a good look at the next Grand National or Golden Horseshoe winner.

Some equine athletes used in research studies, however, have unexpectedly been found to have mostly fast-twitch fibres whilst having the more rangy conformation of stayers or endurance horses; in such cases, the muscle type has been more influential than the conformation in the type of work the horses have proved best at. For example, visual assessment might have caused observers to select certain horses for long-distance racing but their muscle type has given them the advantage of both fast-twitch muscles and ground-eating conformation. Specific training and exercise techniques can change the proportions of muscle fibre types in an individual horse to some extent, but they can never change a true stayer into a sprinter or vice versa.

The tendons which work with muscles are a frequent source of injury in athletic horses. As modified muscle tissue, they, too, are composed mainly of protein (collagen) and also have groups of fibrils bundled together to form tendon fibres surrounded by a membrane called the tendon sheath.

Tendons are not actually elastic, as is often thought, they have a crimped texture to the fibres like a coiled spring rather than true elastic stretch. Under tension, the 'spring' or crimped structure is partly straightened out but recoils when weight is taken off the tendon again as, for example, a leg is lifted at the end of a step. In this way, tendons act as a free energy store as the recoil mechanism makes use of gravity, not energy, and of the tissues' natural inclination to return to their normal configuration, so giving the horse an extra push off the ground.

The thicker the tendons the stronger they are because the fibre diameters are greater, but the longer the tendons the weaker they are because the length of the long cannon bone, for instance, which goes with long tendons increases the leverage effect and the thinner tendon has to move a greater weight or cope with a greater force over a longer distance. Given two sticks of the same diameter, it is easier to snap the longer one than the shorter one. If a horse has long cannon bones, therefore, make sure that he has thick tendons to compensate.

Nervous control of movement

Movement happens when, for example, one group of muscles acts to bring a leg forward. Its opposing group begins to contract to control that forward movement and then to bring the leg back. As it reaches the limit of its step, the first group of muscles contracts to control the backward movement and to bring the leg forward again, and so it goes on. But what process actually stimulates the muscles to contract and cause movement in the first place? This is the job of the horse's highly complex nervous system, the 'headquarters' of which are the brain and spinal cord.

The nervous system has two main parts: the central nervous system (CNS – the brain and spinal cord) and the peripheral nervous system (PNS – the nerves branching from the spinal cord). Together these are called the somatic nervous system and control the horse's voluntary actions and, therefore, his voluntary/skeletal muscle function. (There are two subdivisions of the PNS responsible for the horse's involuntary movements, among other things, which do not concern us in relation to conformation and action.)

The three tasks of the somatic nervous system are as follows:

- It must detect, via the horse's senses, what is happening around and to him in the way of pressure, pain, heat, cold, weather conditions, the approach of danger, hunger, thirst and so on. It must then send 'intelligence' (information messages) by means of chemicals and/or electrical nervous impulses along sensory or 'feeling' nerves to the brain and/or the spinal cord.
- The CNS must decide what to do about the information received.
- If movement is felt to be appropriate, it must send messages back along motor ('action') nerves to the muscles to contract and so move the horse or part of him.

As far as initiating movement is concerned, the horse first decides to move, for whatever reason. He may hear a vocal request or feel a squeeze or kick in the ribs from his rider, a twitch of the rein or a jab on the bit, a flick or a cut from the whip, a dig from the spurs or just a little nudge from the seat or a simple shift of weight. He may simply decide that he wants to see what is happening on the other side of the field or find out which horse is standing behind the field shelter, or he may be out on a hack and decide to go home no matter what his rider does to try to stop him. He may have some other sort of physical stimulus such as feeling thirsty which will prompt him to move over to the water source.

The overall view of movement

Now that we have considered the skeleton, the muscles, the very basic ABC of locomotion and the similarly basic nervous initiation of movement, it might be interesting to decide which of the three is most important in making a horse an effective mover within his particular equestrian discipline – that is, for a specific job or purpose. Is it:

- his basic framework (his skeleton, which does, after all, control his foundation shape)
- his muscular development and, particularly, type

(slow-twitch or fast-twitch) which are major influences on the type of work he can do
- the efficiency of the nervous process which controls it all

There are many variables in a horse's action which mix together like the ingredients of a cake: no one ingredient represents the determining factor. We have to consider the natural length and scope of the horse's stride, his agility and co-ordination, whether or not his gait is true and straight or shows deviations or actual interferences, and the speed or tempo of his steps. The final answer to the question might surprise you!

Skeletal framework

For good general balance, we require a horse who, when mature, is of equal height at withers and croup; this is a physical parameter which has traditionally always been honoured.

Horses who are croup-high, however, and with a hindquarter/pelvis which slopes downwards somewhat from the croup to the root of the tail are often favoured for sprint racing, showjumping and draught/carriage work because of the extra length and leverage (strength and power) exerted by the longer bones which lengthen the hindleg, and the ability to bring the hindlegs well forward under the body for length of stride, push from behind and 'drive'. Conversely, a noticeably more 'uphill' conformation may be sought in dressage horses (along with a neck set high on the front of the shoulders and with a natural, upward arch to it), as this make and shape facilitates getting the horse 'in hand' and collected.

A horse who is a little high in front and who also has a long, sloping, well laid back shoulder (from the point of the shoulder at the front up and back to the top of the shoulder blade just below the withers), with good muscular development, should be able to withstand the considerable shock of landing from steeplechase fences or the obstacles met with in top-level eventing. The traditional, ideal angle is no more than 45° (in other words, the shoulder blade – gauged from the ridge running the length of it – should approach the horizontal rather than the vertical in a horse intended for ridden work), but although studies done in North America agree with this, they have also shown that a pastern angle identical to that of the shoulder, as has always been thought to be important, is irrelevant to performance ability. We should not, however, get carried away by checking the angle of an imaginary straight line run from the highest point of the withers to the highest point of the croup, because the height of each is governed largely by the length of the spinous processes of the vertebrae of the withers and sacrum; the precise shape of the ilia of the pelvis to which the sacrum is attached also plays a part in the height of the croup.

The points we should really be scrutinising for this evaluation and the effects we believe it has on the length of a horse's stride and, therefore, his range of motion, are the hip joint and the rotation point of the shoulder blade.

The location of the hip joint (not the outermost point of the wings of the pelvic ilia which horse people call the 'point of hip') can be determined by focusing the eyes on the horse's point of buttock (the tuber ischium or pin bone) and looking forwards a few inches on a horizontal line to the inward dip of the flank below and slightly behind the point of hip. This is the site of the actual hip joint inside the hindquarters.

The scapula, as we have seen, is joined by soft tissue only to the ribcage and has a point around which it rotates or swings back and forth. This rotation point can only be seen when the horse is in action and is easiest spotted, in my experience, in an extended or fast canter or gallop. Watch the horse moving, ideally at liberty, and try to absorb the swing of the shoulder blade, then decide at which point its forward and

An example of croup high conformation where it is not advantageous – in a riding pony. This conformation feature can cause difficulties in saddle fitting as the saddle is constantly inclined to ride forwards and dig into the back of the shoulders and elbows

backward movement meet: as the foreleg stretches forward, the bottom of the shoulder blade comes forward (with the leg obviously attached to the bottom of it) and the top goes backward towards the withers. There must be one point, therefore, which only rotates without actually changing its forward or backward position. This is the rotation point to mark mentally.

The nearer is this point to the withers, the longer the swing of the lower part of the shoulder blade and therefore the longer the reach of the foreleg. For speed, reach or scope, the rotation point should be no less than one-third the length of the scapula down from the top of it; in other words, it should be at the bottom of the top third of the scapula or higher. For such jobs as speed jumping, polo, cutting cattle, gymkhana games and anything requiring nippy, agile movement, the rotation point should be within the second third of the scapula, as this will shorten and quicken the stride in front.

The next step is to have the horse stand still again; now imagine a straight line running from the rotation point of the scapula to the site of the hip joint and decide which end of the line is higher, if either. This, rather than the relative heights of croup and withers, will tell you whether the horse is truly 'uphill' or 'downhill' in his conformation and balance and will give you a good idea of at least one important pointer as to how he will move, how he will feel, how easy he will be to train for the job you have in mind and how effortlessly or otherwise he might perform it.

Other factors to be considered include:

- The length of bones and, therefore, the leverage they are able to exert. Longer bones in the upper

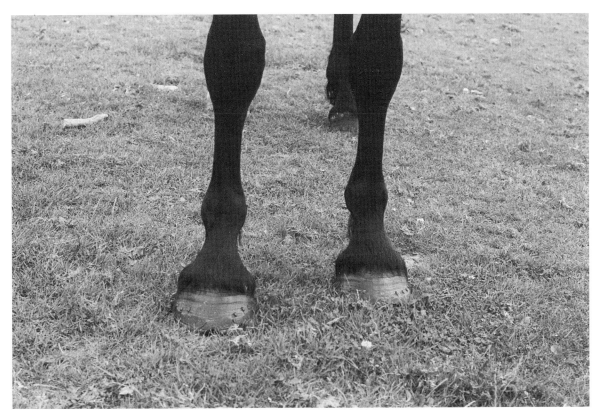

Good, straight legs on a Welsh Cob. Note the particularly strong looking, shield-shaped knees and generous feet

legs, for instance, not only give a longer, more sweeping stride but also greater thrust.

- The manner and place in which a horse puts his feet down. The action should be what we call straight, with the hoofprints all aligned in the same plane, which makes for the most energy-efficient movement; if the prints are out of alignment, there is a deviation in action which means the leg is travelling away from the straight plane, travelling further than it should and so consuming more energy than it otherwise would. Repeated stride after stride, this is a significant factor to consider, not to mention the fact that horses with crooked action are more likely to kick and injure themselves and that legs which are not placed down straight and true experience uneven forces up them, which also causes injury.

  It should be borne in mind that legs can travel outside the normal, straight plane of movement but return to it before or as the foot lands; therefore, the hoofprint will be in the right place but the horse will still have a crooked, not a straight, action.

- Whether or not the horse over-tracks (places his hindfeet in front of the preceding forefoot prints) or tracks up (places the hindfeet in the same spot as the forefoot prints). Horses should over-track in walk and track up in trot.

- The natural speed at which a horse is most comfortable moving in each gait. Each gait has an energy-efficient gear, a 'cruising' speed in that gait at which it is easiest for the horse to move and at which he consumes the least oxygen and energy. The higher a horse's cruising speed in each gait the faster he will be and vice versa. Higher cruising speeds enable horses to cover the miles faster, with minimal use of energy and it is therefore longer before fatigue sets in.

  Making a horse work above and below his cruising speed, as is done much of the time in competitive dressage, schooling at home and so on, may advance his training as far as technique is concerned and will develop muscle (the right musculature or the wrong musculature depending on whether or not he is ridden and trained to use himself correctly or incorrectly) but it uses up considerable energy which is why it is such hard work for the horse – a fact which is often overlooked but which is plainly shown by the horse's sweating and raised pulse and respiration rates.

- The length of the horse's spine. This has a significant influence on whether or not he is agile or ungainly; over-long backs make for lumbering movement and over-short ones for stiffness and a proneness to over-reach injuries.

- The length of his neck relative to his body. The head and neck are the horse's natural 'balancing pole'. A long, low neck ending in a heavy head will put a horse permanently 'on the forehand' and make it difficult for him to work in a well-balanced way, and especially to collect, whereas a very short neck with a small, light head may make him nippy as far as his limbs are concerned but not very well balanced or agile overall.

  Domestic horses, however, nearly all have longer necks and smaller heads than their primitive ancestors because we have selectively bred for this characteristic of (to us) beauty and balance in movement.

Musculature

The same principle of leverage and movement around a rotation point applies to the attachment points of muscles. Although muscles always attach at more or less the same place on bones, if they have their origin high up a bone, this will result in a longer and perhaps more scopey stride because the bone's fulcrum is high, so the movement below it is bigger and the stride more far-reaching. Try holding a pencil at the top between your thumb and finger and move them slightly to make the bottom end of the pencil move sideways. If you now hold the pencil further down, you have to move your thumb and finger much more to obtain the same amount of movement at the bottom. So the further down a bone the muscles originate the shorter and usually the higher the horse's stride. A longer stride confers speed but a lower muscle origin, with a shorter stride, is a stronger structure and is useful for power work such as jumping, higher levels of dressage and draught.

The type of fibre a muscle contains is also obviously relevant, as we have seen. Although a horse is born with a set number of muscle fibres of different types and this number cannot be changed, the efficiency of the different types can be increased by appropriate fitness training, basically by building up the horse's fitness and working him at the speed and for the distances and time required for the competition in mind. This does not mean that a sprinter can be converted into an endurance horse, for example, or vice versa, but it does mean that his capacity for a particular type of work can at least be increased.

It is interesting to note that if a horse's skeletal structure does not make him appear promising for a particular job, his ability to perform that type of work better can at least be enhanced by appropriate fitness training and development of the right sort of muscle fibres. To get peak performance from any horse, though, it is far more

The horse's power source is his hindquarters. They should look balanced, muscular and uncompromising, like this, with two vertical hindlegs supporting them. The thighs should be the same width as the hips in a normally-muscled horse (allowing for condition) and the whole picture from behind should present a feeling of irresistible power

logical and effective to train him for the type of work for which he is best suited.

Nervous control

Muscles can only contract and therefore move bones when they receive messages from the nervous system. Like humans and other animals, horses differ in their individual mental and physical make-up, some being highly reactive, with lightning-quick responses, and others being much slower to respond. Hundreds of thousands of nerve cells, under the control of the central nervous system, are involved in initiating a single muscle movement. The horse's actions must become, in a way, semi-involuntary, so that he does not have to think about every step he takes, particularly when working at speed, and his natural sense of proprioception (knowing without having to look where each part of his body is, what it is doing and how it is feeling) plays a big part in his movement and maintenance of balance. The CNS responds to the messages it continually receives by this means. The initiation of movement of each muscle fibre or cell, the co-ordination of the opposing muscle groups and the complementary muscles themselves, the speed with which messages are relayed to and from the CNS and therefore the ultimate strength, power, speed, agility and basic response of the horse himself are all first and foremost under the control of his nervous system – his 'hard wiring'.

Although horses can be trained to improve their movement and can have their muscles developed to change their way of going, their basic action and its elegance or clumsiness are all determined by the type and efficiency of their nervous control – and this is inherited from their ancestors. Some humans make beautifully graceful dancers whereas others will always have two left feet and no sense of rhythm! Horses are no different.

Nervous performance, though, can be 'trained'. Think how difficult you first found it to, say, ride a bicycle, drive a car, type, play an instrument – or ride a horse. You probably thought you would never do it, but by constant repetition the movements necessary to effective performance became ingrained in your subconscious and ultimately you became competent and improved, without even having to think about it. This is what happens with horses. Training can enhance the performance of the nervous system as it can any other, but the raw material to work with has to be there in the first place. You will never turn a natural sluggard into a lightning-quick reactor or vice versa but you can bring about a certain amount of change.

Everyone involved at all intensively with horses knows that the best-conformed horses are not always the best movers and that some animals which are singularly unimpressive when standing still light up once they move. Likewise, in in-hand classes (at halter in the U.S.A.) they by no means always go on to win in harness or under saddle. In fact, most do not seem to do so. It is obvious that there are several inherent factors involved in the physical performance of a horse and there are also others such as the horse's emotional state, the management and horsemanship skills of his trainer and rider or driver, the weather, farriery – which is absolutely crucial – nutrition and other nuances of environment and spirituality.

The three topics we have considered are closely linked and of the three, the type and effectiveness of his nervous control is probably the most important, then his musculature and finally his actual conformation.

How injuries affect conformation and action

Horses are athletic animals who frequently sustain injuries, mainly during their work but also in stable and field. Their bodies react to pain in just the same way as ours do: the horse, on experiencing pain, will start to move his body in such a way as to avoid placing stress on the painful part – he compensates for the painful action by moving differently. This different, compensatory movement is usually an unnatural action for him, which puts stresses on other parts of the body in ways in which they were not designed to experience it.

If you have had an injury as common and basic as a sprained ankle, for instance, you will know how debilitating and exhausting it can be to compensate physically for the fact that you cannot bear to put your foot on the ground or take any significant weight on the painful joint. You place more weight on your sound leg, which comes under a great deal of stress as a result. But that is not all. You soon become aware of other stresses and strains, particularly on your back as you use its muscles (and, of course, their associated tendons and ligaments) in unaccustomed ways to rebalance your weight. The sound muscles in your injured leg and lower torso will be used, unusually, to keep the leg (about 25 per cent of your bodyweight) permanently lifted off the ground to avoid hurting your ankle further.

These soft tissue structures were never designed to perform these sorts of actions and bear these sorts of peculiar stresses and may well, in a short time, become overstressed and injured themselves. Meanwhile, the muscles of your injured leg which are used in normal walking and running become weaker fairly quickly, even to the point of noticeably atrophying (shrinking) due to lack of use – and before long you're in a pretty bad way!

The road to recovery is not a short, straight one, either. Not only do the injured tissues of your ankle, and possibly your other leg and your back, have to repair, but the unused tissues in these parts of your body plus those in your injured leg eventually have to be built up again, which takes time.

The above description shows how injury affects and debilitates the body, whether it is human or equine; horses are made of just the same kind of skin, flesh and bone as humans or any other animals and feel the pain, stresses and strains in just the same way, so relating our own injuries to those of our horses may remind us what an injured horse will be feeling like. Athletic horses are recognised for fairly frequently sustaining leg injuries (tendon injuries of the forelegs are, for example, particularly common in racehorses and horses which jump high or at speed), but I find that very many horses also have back injuries which go unrecognised or, sadly, are not accepted as such by their owners. Back problems do not always cause actual lameness but they usually cause difficult behaviour in the form of either general resistances or specific problems during work.

Any minor injury which is not recognised, accepted and treated may still heal naturally in time, even if the horse is still able to work, but it is likely to change the horse's action permanently so that his initially compensatory action becomes habitual. The horse may develop the ingrained habit of moving in a certain way after healing has taken place because he remembers how painful his foot, leg, neck or back once was and he does not want to experience that again,

or there may be some retained weakness or very slight pain or discomfort which is enough to change his natural, pre-injury action. This is why rehabilitation, usually in the form of specific, controlled exercise and sometimes physiotherapy, is needed after injury, to re-educate the muscles to work properly and naturally.

An incorrect type of movement can change his appearance because, as I have said, certain muscles will atrophy and others will develop as his action changes. In some cases, this can actually change his skeleton because he holds himself in a different way and the bone reshapes or remodels to accommodate the changed forces. Horses which have sustained repeated tendon or ligament injuries of the legs, usually the

The dipped spine of this Welsh pony, who is in his 30s, is purely due to old age and years of the combined effects of resisting gravity and carrying weight – that of riders above and of his own abdominal contents below

forelegs, sometimes develop 'dropped fetlocks' because of the weakened soft tissue structures, which can no longer support the legs to the same extent. Another conformation change occurs when horses, often old horses who have worked hard, become 'over at the knee' so that the knees appear to knuckle over forward slightly when viewed from the side, because of stresses on the knee joints.

A conformational change which occurs to the back in older horses is that the spine dips and the back therefore sags owing to a lifetime of not only carrying the great weight of the horse's own abdominal contents slung from underneath the spine but also that of various riders over the years. Broodmares who have had many foals develop this feature late in life for similar reasons: a foetus, at least in the latter months of pregnancy, is heavy and, unlike a rider who dismounts after a relatively short time, the broodmare can obtain no lasting relief from this extra weight until her foal is born.

How injuries happen

There are very many ways in which horses sustain injuries, some of which we may not even have considered.

- They can experience knocks, bruises, cuts and so on in the general course of life. Treading on a stone in the field can bruise a foot, slipping on muddy ground or ice can wrench the soft tissues of the back and legs and becoming cast in the stable can do the same; cuts and tears can easily occur from sharp nails sticking out of buildings or from barbed wire on fencing.

- Tendons and ligaments can be 'pulled' by having too much stress placed on them. Tendons and ligaments are often damaged by overstretching caused by inco-ordination as a result of fatigue of the associated parent muscle (in the case of tendons) in the upper leg; this happens when horses are worked too hard or for too long for their state of fitness.

- Anything which causes the horse pain and discomfort and which he naturally compensates for

An ill-fitting, uncomfortable saddle (this one is pressing around the withers) always causes a horse to tense the neck and shoulders, lower the back and belly and trail the hindquarters and legs. Compensating for the discomfort the saddle causes, the horse uses his musculature wrongly and unnaturally which can result in stress and injury

by moving unnaturally can cause injury. This includes poor rider technique, work evasion and badly fitting and inappropriately adjusted tack and harness, including clothing.

- A fall in the field, stable, yard or horsebox, or during work, can be very traumatic for a horse or pony because they are such heavy animals and hit the ground with much more force than we do.
- Kicks, treads and bites can all be administered by one horse to another and, sadly, some horses are deliberately injured by their riders or handlers. One form of abuse is the incorrect or over-use of training aids or 'gadgets' which force the horse into an unnatural outline and can cause injury.
- Concussion from working on hard ground or kicking and pawing in the stable can cause tiny fractures of bone, damage cartilage and disturb soft tissues.
- Over-soft or deep, muddy going causes stress on the body because they involve more effort than usual, and inconsistent *manège* and gallop surfaces (badly formulated and poorly maintained) cause stride inco-ordination and possibly concussion and slipping if the horse goes through the top material to the base below.
- Lack of attention to the teeth and subsequent resistance to bit and bridle in work are often unrecognised causes of muscular injury which, by causing stiffness in the jaw and poll, can spread throughout the body.
- Badly balanced, maintained and shod feet greatly affect a horse's comfort and the quality of his stride and gait. If he puts his feet down in a self-protective way or disregards his discomfort and works on anyway, injury can easily follow, owing to uneven stresses or unnatural, compensatory action.
- Finally, poor conformation can itself cause injury because of uneven or less than optimal distribution of forces on the body, a subject discussed in Chapter 4.

Healing of soft tissue

Unfortunately, the healing of injuries is one area in which Nature is far from perfect; she simply achieves the best standard she can according to our current stage of evolution. This is what happens:

1 When an injury occurs, tissues are broken down and fluids, including blood, seep into the surrounding area congesting it. There is inflammation, involving swelling, heat, pressure on nerves, toxic substances and perhaps some irritation caused by macrophages or 'clear-up' cells which arrive to remove damaged tissues, and the blood starts to clot around the injury. All this creates pain and loss of use of the injured area.

2 Pain causes muscle spasm. We all 'clam up' when we are frightened, in pain (which itself causes fear), cold or nervous.

3 Tight muscles squeeze and narrow the blood vessels passing through them, resulting in reduced circulation, which means less oxygen and fewer nutrients being delivered to the tissues and fewer toxic waste products of metabolism being removed. This creates an unhealthy environment in which the muscle cannot thrive.

4 The muscles therefore atrophy and become weak.

5 Muscle weakness causes strain on tendons and ligaments.

6 This further pain and discomfort causes loss of movement.

7 Adhesions then form. These are fibrous tissue joins between two surfaces which are normally separate and slide over each other. In the case of an injured tendon, for example, adhesions may form between the tendon and its protective outer sheath through which it slides. If the injury is next to a bone, adhesions may even calcify and become bony.

8 When the horse moves, the adhesions themselves hamper movement and cause the horse discomfort or further pain, particularly if they themselves tear, creating further injury. And so the process continues in a vicious circle.

After about a week, new blood vessels begin to develop in the injured tissue, restoring circulation, and specialised cells arrive to patch up and repair the damage as best they can. Eventually, the original injury and any subsequent ones caused by adhesions will reach a level of complete healing but the tissue produced in place of the original healthy cells is called a cicatrix or scar tissue. This is fibrous tissue which does not have the qualities of the original and is more prone to further injury. Often, there is some loss of the original form and function of the structure concerned. The horse may then be permanently disabled, mildly or seriously, and will be unable to work at his previous levels. For instance, injured tendons and ligaments never heal to the strength and function they had formerly and the horse is usually retired to a less demanding job. If he is not and is worked at his previous levels, he usually sustains a further injury quite soon which will certainly put paid to his career in that particular discipline.

With proper treatment of an injury, the sequence is rather different:

1 When an injury occurs, the horse feels pain.
2 Appropriate treatment reduces the pain. This would comprise veterinary treatment, probably involving box rest, painkillers and anti-inflammatory drugs, and possibly also physical therapy and a suitable rehabilitation programme of controlled exercise.
3 Lack of pain means lack of muscle spasm.
4 No muscle spasm means no interruption to the blood circulation through the tissues.
5 Therefore there is minimal muscle atrophy and loss of strength.
6 There is no ligament strain as a result.
7 There is minimal consequent loss of normal movement.
8 Therefore there is little or no formation of scar tissue and adhesions, and so no re-injury.

Better recovery takes place than if things had been left to Nature but even so it may take several weeks, months or even more than a year depending on the tissue involved, the age and health of the horse, its management and diet, the quality of the blood supply and the severity of the injury. If infection sets in, recovery will take longer. Also, working the horse (as opposed to giving him rehabilitation exercise) before recovery will simply result in fresh injury.

Healing of bone tissue

Bone heals better than any other tissue in the body. Of course, if a leg is badly shattered the horse may have to be put down even though, technically, it would be possible to repair it; the horse's weight and behaviour is frequently against him – we cannot tell him to keep weight off an injured bone and to keep still, and why! By their very nature, many horses panic when injured and many thrash around and charge about the recovery box when coming round after an operation, undoing all the vet's good work. However, techniques, anaesthetics, sedatives and so on are improving all the time and many bad fractures (the correct word for a break) which previously would have meant certain euthanasia can now offer good hope of repair.

When a fracture occurs, the bone ends have to be brought together for a good repair. In nature this does not usually happen. A few feral equidae have been reported which have obviously had broken bones and, amazingly, survived because a massive callus of bony tissue has formed naturally around the break, leaving an obvious deformity. This would only happen in areas free from natural predators, as otherwise the horse would be killed long before recovery could take place. If his galloping ability were reduced after the repair, this would also clearly affect his survival chances if predators were in the area. Grazing and generally surviving on three legs is also extremely difficult for an outdoor, grazing, running animal, although it has happened, if apparently rarely. Basically, bone heals as follows:

1 Blood from damaged blood vessels surrounds the fracture and begins to clot.
2 Special cells of fibrous tissue start to knit tissue together and a callus forms from this tissue and from cartilage cells and immature bone cells which secrete bone tissue. This callus replaces the clotted blood and acts like a tough but not rigid splint to help reduce movement of the injured area and so assist healing.

3 The callus becomes calcified or bony.
4 Finally, the callus reorganises itself into typical bone.

Repair can take place as soon as six weeks in a young animal and often there is no sign of a break. In older horses, repair can take from six months to a year or so. The quality of repair obviously depends on the degree of damage and the amount of correction needed, the horse's age, diet, blood supply and temperament (whether or not he is a 'good patient') and whether or not the site can be kept infection-free.

If too much stress (weight, or traction from movement) is placed on the injury due to tendon and ligament attachment to and action on it, resulting in poor immobilisation, the repair will not be so good; the callus will still form but may not fully calcify, remaining partly composed of fibrous tissue. This makes for a weak repair.

If the injury does not heal well, there may be a permanent lump around it which affects a horse's appearance, at least, and if the repair is on or near a joint, it may interfere with its function and therefore the horse's action. Several racing and competition stallions have survived fractures and been retired to stud and good mares can become broodmares if their injury does not make life difficult. Geldings are often put down for economic reasons unless they are lucky enough to have owners who will keep them as pets or companions, or even as hacks if they are sound but not up to hard work. Indeed, because fractures and injuries which take a long time to heal are expensive to cope with, many horses who sustain such injuries are put down to save costs.

Physiotherapy and other modalities

Today, physiotherapy is well established as a healing aid in the horse world and a common adjunct to veterinary treatment in the healing of injuries. Physiotherapists may use various healing techniques and machines such as laser therapy, ultrasound, electromagnetism, interferential therapy (for deep tissue injuries), hot and cold therapy, massage and others. Physiotherapists, and indeed all animal therapists in the U.K., must work through veterinary referral (the law is different in some other countries), but most are qualified and highly skilled therapists in their own right with administrative bodies controlling their registration. Physical therapists such as sports massage therapists, shiatsu practitioners (shiatsu being an ancient energy therapy akin to acupressure, also comprising gentle physical therapy), homeopaths (a few of whom are vets themselves), herbalists, chiropractors, osteopaths, acupuncturists, aromatherapists and others can all play a part, as appropriate, in helping horses to recover from injury or simply withstand the rigours of being an athletic, working animal.

Most vets are now happy to allow other competent therapists to apply their skills for the benefit of horses. Not every therapy or form of medicine, including the orthodox, has the answer for every situation and some will succeed where others fail; this makes it all the more encouraging that complementary medicine and therapies, many of which are highly effective in my experience, are much more widely available and accepted and can be used along with conventional veterinary treatment.

CHAPTER

4

STRESS AND STRAIN

Because the horse evolved to be an efficient galloper and was meant to be gently on the move most of his time with occasional bursts of speed when needed, his body is well formed and structured to take the normal stresses and strains of such a lifestyle. We tend to think that we have 'improved' the domesticated equine athlete structurally and know a lot about getting him fit for his work, and that he can therefore easily withstand the extra work we ask him to do and the extra forces we thereby apply to his bones, muscles, tendons, ligaments and other tissues. This is not so, however, as evidenced by the high number of injuries domesticated horses sustain as a direct result of their work.

Poor conformation can certainly increase a horse's or pony's chances of being injured because it may represent a weakness in his structure, an uneven, unnatural direction of forces up his legs and through his body which puts his tissues, bony or soft, under an unbearable strain. Let us look at how the body receives and distributes forces when the horse is in action. There is a basic tenet of physics which applies to everything physical and certainly to horses and their work: force equals mass (simply translated as weight) times acceleration (simply translated as speed, not *increasing* speed as non-physicists might think). Put even more simply and applied to horses, this rule means that speed and weight are the main 'killers' of athletic horses. The faster a

horse is required to go and the more weight he is asked to carry or pull, the more force this amounts to and the more chance his body has of suffering over-stress or distress resulting in torn soft tissues or fractured (chipped or broken) bone or cartilage tissue.

Most horses can move around relatively slowly, even carrying a significant weight, for several hours without coming to any harm, but ask them to carry that same weight at speed across country, round a racecourse or even on a training gallop, pleasure ride or active hack and not only will they run out of energy fairly quickly because it is hard work, but also the stresses of the weight on their bodies will be compounded by the speed, so injury is likely to occur.

Something else which needs to be borne in mind, although it is really outside the scope of this book, is that fatigued tissues become that way because the bloodstream cannot deliver nutrients and oxygen for the creation of energy, or remove the waste products which result, fast enough for the needs of a horse working hard at speed. This type of work is called anaerobic (which means 'without oxygen') because it has to be done without sufficient or any oxygen; a by-product of this process is toxic lactic acid which creates an over-acidic, unfriendly environment in the muscles, causing injury to muscle tissue. Horses can also, of course, work hard if not terribly fast for several hours and also end up exhausted.

The stresses of a stride

The horse's thrusting power comes almost entirely from his hindquarters and hindlegs if he is moving correctly, and is not compensating for pain, restricting harness or tack or a poor rider, all of which prevent him moving properly. The job of the forelegs is to carry the force and the weight of the forehand, not to haul the horse along with the shoulder and forearm muscles, although some horses with back, hindquarter or hindleg discomfort or restrictive riders learn to

This triptych shows the basic direction of forces on the horse's legs and spine during action. As a hindleg impacts with the ground, the force travels up the hindleg and into the spine at the pelvis via the hip joint. It travels forwards along the spine and peters out (having been dissipated along the way by soft tissues and joint flexions). As the foreleg impacts, force travels up the foreleg and shoulder and is mainly absorbed by the thoracic sling although the forelimb joints absorb a good deal of it as do the soft tissues of the leg

do this and develop the 'wrong' muscles as a result. Horses who are not trained to use their bodies correctly and protectively under weight (dealt with on page 62 under 'Tack and harness' and in Chapter 6) may also develop this way of going.

The horse's tendons help a little by storing some energy in their crimped fibre structure and releasing it when a leg is angled backward at the end of a stride. This quality, however, is limited and is often abused, which is why tendons not infrequently tear or even snap under severe stress. If it were not for this 'walking on springs' effect, all horses would be awful, bone-jarring rides; indeed older, hard-worked or frequently injured horses sometimes lose this spring to their step.

Provided they are standing in a reasonably balanced way, horses start their strides with their hindlegs. A leg will come forward; this involves flexing its joints to lift it up and clear the ground as its muscles, mainly the muscles in the upper leg, bring it forward. Flexor muscles, mainly around the back of the upper leg bones contract and extensors mainly around the front, take over to move the leg forward. The muscles are attached at their origins to particular bones, and the tendons running from their lower ends attach to other bones at their insertions. Therefore, when the muscle shortens or contracts this produces a force on the muscle tissue and a pull or force on the tendon, which must likewise pull with it the bone to which it is attached. This also creates a force on the tissues at the point of attachment. The joint between the muscle/tendon unit's two bones flexes or bends, creating some movement and wear on the cartilage and other tissues, and the leg is picked up. This is a very over-simplified description, and there are several muscles, tendons, bones and joints involved in each step.

As the leg is picked up to clear the ground, extensor muscles take over and contract to pull the leg forward. The leg straightens out forwards and the hoof hits the ground. The concussion or jar that this generates travels partly down into the ground but mainly up the path of least resistance, i.e. the horse's leg, lessening as it travels upwards. The foot obviously receives the greatest force of impact, followed by the lower leg and so on. The joints of the hindleg flex or 'give' a little immediately after impact, stretching the associated tendons to a greater or lesser extent, depending on the force received (determined by speed and weight), which absorbs and dissipates some concussion. Then other muscles take over and extend the leg out backwards, using the ground as a pushing board to heave the horse's weight forwards. The tendons' elastic recoil mechanism now gives the horse a slight energy-free boost forward and upward by being enabled to spring back to its normal crimped structure as the leg is relieved of weight.

The force of the stride travels up the leg and, via the hip joint at the top of the thigh bone and the pelvis, passes to the sacrum and forward along the spine. As this is happening, the corresponding foreleg is reaching out forward to catch the forehand and, by stiffening the knee but flexing the joints at the point of the shoulder, elbow, fetlock and foot, it provides both rigid support in the middle like the spoke of a wheel and also jar-absorbing flexion at its extremities.

As we have seen, there is no bony joint between the shoulder and ribcage, the chest or thorax being slung between the shoulder blades, mainly by muscle but also by other soft tissues which bind the bones in place and allow the chest to sink slightly, again to absorb impact, as the foreleg hits the ground. This thoracic sling, as it is called, absorbs most of the shock of the decreasing force travelling forward along the spine but also that coming up the leg from the ground as the fore hoof hits it.

The fetlock flexes greatly, the more so the faster the horse is going, the harder he hits the ground (for example, as from a drop fence) and the heavier the weight he is carrying. The body continues forward and the foreleg is angled back to its maximum. At the precise moment when the leg must lift up to prepare for the next stride, the elastic recoil in the tendon comes into play as in the hindleg and bounces the horse onward a little.

Driving horses experience very similar stresses and forces to riding horses as far as their direction up and down the legs and along the spine are concerned, but instead of carrying weight they are pushing it with their hindquarters and hindlegs into some kind of harness (neck collar or breast harness) in order to draw behind them a vehicle carrying weight. Of course, although we say that they are pulling a vehicle, they could only actually do that by having it tied to their tails. The action is that of pushing weight into their shoulders, like a man pushing a wardrobe to move it, and this can put much more stress on their hindlegs, their hindquarters and, in a different way, their backs than that experienced by riding horses. Driving horses, especially the heavy types who haul great weights as in agriculture or heavy transport (and they are still common in many countries) often get curbs (torn plantar ligaments) just below the point of the hock, and sidebones (ossification or 'turning to bone' of the lateral cartilages at the sides of the hindfeet) plus muscle injuries of the hindquarters and backs.

Some countries still delight in pulling contests which in my view are grossly unfair, and which frequently result in serious injuries to the horses who are asked to move excessive dead weights flat on the ground (without wheels). Of course, all equestrian sports can result in cruelty if our demands on the horses are unreasonable.

Ground conditions – Help or hindrance?

The state of the ground has some effect on a horse's stride. The harder the ground the less concussion is absorbed by it and the more by the horse's legs and body, so the greater the chance of concussion injuries and of tissues being damaged because there is no relief on them from force being absorbed by the ground. Comfortably yielding ground such as good turf (the optimal, natural ground surface for horses, as opposed to asses and zebras) or a suitable, prepared riding surface is safest. Over-soft ground may provide more give and absorption but it needs more physical effort and muscular contraction, and therefore pull on the tendons, to

get the leg up out of the ground again, to lift it higher than normal to avoid the ground itself and to stretch it out again from that position.

The horse's way of going has been minutely honed over millions of years and his conformation geared in synchrony with it; it is a very efficient method of motion for a four-legged running animal of his make, shape and foot design. Donkeys and zebras have more upright, boxy feet adapted to harder, drier going such as they experience in their natural habitats (both being desert and semi-desert or scrubland animals), but horses mainly evolved in areas where grasses formed an absorptive root-mat below the surface and developed legs and feet ideally adapted to that ground. That hard-to-find classic, old turf is always the best surface for horses and the physical protection it provides is the main reason that horse paddocks should never be ploughed up unless it is absolutely essential; it destroys the root-mat which takes many years to regenerate. No artificial surface yet devised has perfectly simulated the mechanical effects of old turf.

The effects of work and stress

We ask our equine athletes to produce physical feats far and above anything they would do in nature as far as combined speed, weight-carrying, jumping and stamina are concerned. Wild and feral equidae do travel over long distances but at their own speed and comfortably within their limits – and they do not carry or push any weight. The only time they exert themselves is when they are being chased by a predator.

If a horse is being used for sports or pleasure, he is under significant stress much of the time when working and training. Therefore, any deviation from perfection in both conformation and action can easily result in physical injury. However, there is no such thing as a perfectly conformed horse and an individual can adapt and compensate consciously, to some extent, for faulty conformation and action. Moreover, his body can compensate, for example by thickening a bone here, developing a muscle or two there, and so on. When looking for a performance horse, however, it is safest to seek as near perfection as you can find.

Legs

If the horse has a crooked action, puts a leg down crookedly, dishes, plaits, wings, hits himself and so on, he is not only wasting energy carrying the leg out of its true, straight path, but also overloading some part of the limb and body further up. It must be said, however, that many authorities feel that provided a horse puts his

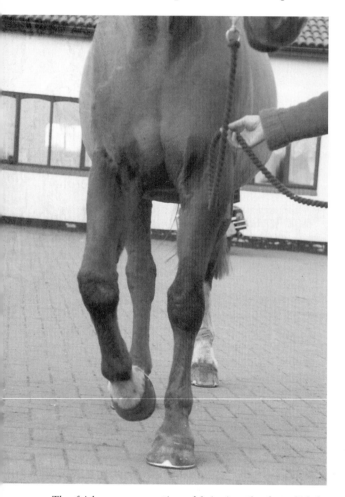

The fairly common action of bringing the foot slightly inwards is an imperfection you can live with provided it is not exaggerated and the horse puts down his feet evenly. No horse is perfect! The author has known several such cases, and other minor action defects, improve with physiotherapy and/or shiatsu treatment

feet down correctly, evenly and in the right place it does not matter much what the leg does when it is in the air, so long as the horse does not hit himself. It may be a waste of a bit of energy, they feel, but correct foot placement will not result in damaging uneven forces on the leg and body, so it is far less important than feet placed and landed wrongly or unevenly. (Some horses are, of course, deliberately bred to dish, that is, to carry the forelegs in a swinging, outward arc which is felt to look showy. All Fino breeds do this and so do many Andalusians and Lusitano horses; in other breeds, however, it is regarded as a fault. You certainly cannot please everybody!)

The horse's legs are not dead straight, like table legs, but 'straight' from the point of view of action as nature intended and the distribution of forces as described above. Anything which deviates from this is a clear disadvantage. Imagine a horse who habitually puts his off foreleg down slightly inwards of the straight-ahead spot where it ought to go, and therefore lands on the outside bearing surface of the hoof first. For an instant during every stride with that leg, the outside bearing surface alone is taking all the weight which should be shared by the whole bearing surface and which is more than nature intended it to take. The leg and body sense that they are being overstressed and try to compensate by producing more horn on the offside quarter and heel of the hoof, more or denser, stronger bone up the outside of the off foreleg, stronger soft tissues to take the extra stress and so on. If this does not happen or if the precise action and weight-bearing function is too much for the horse's make and shape, injury can occur. The bone is constantly slightly crushed by the excess weight up that side of the leg and on the inside of the leg there may be some stretching of the soft tissues, causing injury involving ligaments, connective tissue, muscles or tendons as the weight finally falls down on to the inside of the bearing surface and up the leg once the foot is on the ground.

Although back pain and discomfort probably cause more problems than many of us realise, it is still problems with legs and feet (which can, in any case, stem from back pain and stiffness) which cause most horses to be retired from work or put down. Most experienced horse people, when assessing a horse, will look at overall balance and symmetry first, then their eyes will immediately go to the legs, looking to see that the horse has a 'straight' leg at each corner! Of course we all know horses have a leg at each corner but what this expression means is that the direction of each leg should form a right angle with the ground, whether viewed from the front, back or sides, and that the horse should therefore be able to stand naturally four-square with a hoof at each corner of a rectangle of which each corner is a right angle. Any deviation from this will exacerbate the stress forces described and create problems.

Excessive stress and strain will result in inflammation, with its familiar heat, swelling, pain and stiffness. If both legs of a pair are identically faulty it is bad enough but the horse will probably find it possible to cope and adjust his action in a balanced way. If only one leg is badly conformed, however, this will create uneven postural compensations with the horse holding himself awkwardly in an effort to balance himself. This in turn will affect the whole of his body (remember the example of the sprained ankle). His other three legs, his back, his shoulders, his hips and his neck, and consequently his head carriage, will all be over-stressed and, in time, probably injured. The injuries will heal after a fashion and, over the years, the horse's whole appearance and way of going will probably alter.

I know a Thoroughbred mare who is in regular work, including jumping, in a teaching yard and who has the most incredible, unevenly conformed forelegs from the knees down. I have been around horses all my life and have never before seen legs quite like hers. It is possible to distinguish her natural conformation from the lumps and bumps which have appeared over the years from the stress and strain of compensating for her defects and one can spend a fascinating, if sad, twenty minutes tracing the story of the state of her legs just by following a logical process of which conformation defect will affect which other area of the leg and body with what

result. To ride, she feels like a rowing boat on a rough sea, lurching her rider not only backwards and forwards but also from side to side. She actually moves more freely and feels more comfortable if she is encouraged to go with energy and some speed. I understand that she is used not only for regular student lessons but also for examinations. She goes sound and is not receiving painkillers. I believe that she is in her mid-teens and she is certainly a remarkable example of how a horse can learn to cope with life and compensate for nature's bad deals, but I admit that if she were mine I would retire and cosset her for the rest of her life! Incidentally, she raced with those legs early in life. Today, she is very useful as an example to students not only of equine adaptation but also as a study in conformation and compensation in action.

Body tissues respond to injury with inflammation and subsequent healing, which may result in fibrous or bony lumps and bumps on the legs or possibly, if tendons or ligaments have been badly sprained (torn), with the familiar 'bowed tendons' or more angular joints because of the

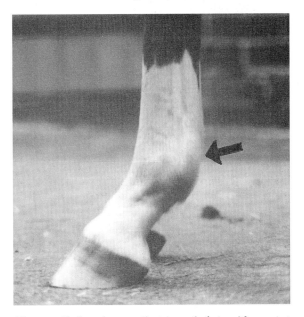

These well-shaped, expertly-trimmed feet with correct foot/pastern axis belong to a Thoroughbred yearling who, unfortunately, already has a tendinous windgall which does not augur well for his future soundness and ability to stand up to training and racing

reduced support provided by the healed tissues. The horse may become over at the knee or down at the fetlocks, for instance. Sometimes extra bone is thrown out by the body, resulting in permanent hard lumps which may or may not interfere with the movement of an associated or nearby joint, and therefore with the horse's action.

Before any treatment or rehabilitation can take place after an injury, it is essential to get an accurate diagnosis from a veterinary surgeon so that everyone, owners and other therapists alike, can be sure what they are dealing with; similar-looking injuries may need different treatment.

The lower legs are subject to many injuries as a result of blows, stresses and strains. Let us take just one site and briefly look at injuries which can occur there, and which horse people usually call a 'splint'. This usually starts as a painful swelling on the inside of the cannon bone, usually of a foreleg. The splint bones are remnants of toes in prehistoric horse ancestors and are still present, bound to the shaft of the main cannon bone by membrane and capable of causing trouble.

Splints are commonly thrown up by concussion which bruises the bone, or by the tearing of a membrane or ligament attached to the bone surface. Bleeding occurs under the membrane lining the bone (the periosteum), from which new bone is formed. This lifts the membrane from the outer surface of the bone, causing the horse a good deal of pain and prompting the formation of a blood clot and fibrous callus. Eventually, this will probably harden into bone or ossify, and the horse will be left with a lump on his leg. Athletically working horses put various stresses on their legs and feet, and torsion (twist) forces can tear ligaments and membranes, lifting them off the bone, with the same results as above but from a different cause.

Another injury occurs when a horse has been kicked at this spot or has banged the leg, fracturing the shaft of the splint bone. Whilst displaying the same symptoms of pain, swelling and inner bleeding, there may be outward signs on the skin of a blow, such as skin and hair damage. An experienced vet may have strong suspicions that the splint bone may be fractured, but can

only tell by having the leg X-rayed. The horse must rest and the fractured ends of the splint bone must meet in order for the callus to form and ossify, so this injury will take longer to heal than the others. Sometimes an operation is needed to remove the severed segment of bone.

Lumps and bumps which appear at joints may be due to osteoarthritis, tiny fractures which have ossified or blows to the area. Sore or 'bucked' shins, which are usually seen in young racehorses, are the results of tiny fractures down the fronts of the cannon bones ossifying and leaving a thickened appearance. Although all these sorts of injuries will affect a horse's looks, only those located so that they hamper joint movement will affect his action. It must be remembered, however, that osteoarthritis (degenerative joint disease or DJD) is a progressive condition, although it can be helped somewhat today by orthodox veterinary medicine, physiotherapy and complementary therapies, including appropriate nutrition.

Any kind of work over and above the sort a horse would do naturally can over-stress his body but it is probably the feet and legs of jumping horses which come in for the greatest loads. Jumping itself is not unnatural to the horse but jumping a great deal, as do our steeplechasers, hurdlers, point-to-pointers, showjumpers and eventers, certainly is. The extreme flexion then extension of the hindlimb joints on take-off taxes them greatly, although the fact that the horse is moving forward already is a help.

The time when the hindlegs come under the greatest strain is when the horse is getting up from the ground and having to hoist his relatively great weight (even for a small pony) up against the force of gravity. Even a slight discomfort or pain, injury or abnormality, will show itself at this time because the several short bones act as levers with only semi-fixed joints rather than as one longer one with no weak links. The ligaments binding and supporting the joints are under maximum stretch and stress as they control the joints, as are the muscles and tendons heaving up the horse's bodyweight. It is therefore good policy always to watch your horse carefully whenever you spot him getting up to make sure he does it easily and comfortably. Any delay, excessive preparation or effort, distressed expression or, particularly, seconds spent in the dog-sit position or swivelling round on the buttocks, spells trouble, as does regular failure to rise at the first attempt without someone hassling him. However, he should never be hurried, as he may become anxious and rise before his position is quite right, stressing his hindlegs even more.

As far as the forelegs are concerned, the landing force on the forefeet of a jumping horse, particularly on the navicular bones and the tendons and ligaments which absorb the force and attempt to prevent overflexion of the lower limb joints, is obviously grossly unnatural. It is not surprising that so many jumping horses have leg problems and that their owners are constantly concerned with examining their horses' legs and with trying to protect them, not to mention choosing horses with as near perfect legs and feet as possible in the first place.

The main problems experienced by jumpers are DJD (osteoarthritis) of the hocks, tendon and ligament sprain and navicular disease in the front legs although there are others, of course. Most of us are foreleg-fixated because we have been told that the horse's forehand carries about two-thirds of his weight, plus that of a rider, a saddle and maybe a weightcloth, and that this weight is compounded when he lands from a jump. We should not forget, however that it is the hindlegs which are the real powerhouse for much of the horse's work and that they also come in for a great deal of stress; the horse is truly a 'rear-wheel drive' animal.

Feet and farriery

I once attended a farriery-cum-veterinary seminar at which delegates were somewhat stunned to hear that about three-quarters of all lameness is in the feet. That does seem a high figure and it is possible that the speaker meant that three-quarters of all lameness is either in the feet or stems from problems with them, which seems more realistic to a lay observer. Over the years various theories arise about feet and shoeing, which both intrigue the horse-owning public and make them feel guilty that they have hitherto been doing things wrong – or rather that their farrier has. 'And you know what farriers are like,' someone will complain. 'They always think owners don't know anything about feet and they don't even listen when you ask about new ideas, or they just pooh-pooh them.' I am afraid there is some truth in that. I find that farriers on the whole are now becoming much more professional in their outlook and more customer-orientated than they used to be, but a good farrier who will discuss things with you, listen to your point of view, consider your questions and explain why he thinks a particular theory or practice is or is not relevant or suitable for your horse and circumstances, is still a fairly rare bird, however.

Before considering the most recent farriery idea to hit the horse world at the time of writing, let us go over the main points of the structure and function of the foot and the traditional way to balance a horse's foot – a method which has been the mainstay of farriery practice for many generations as a base point from which some deviations may be made according to an individual horse's needs or his natural or induced make, shape and action.

The hoof developed from the blunt, almost claw-like little hooves on the toes of the modern horse's multi-toed ancestors. The wall of the hoof round the outside of the foot is made of dead horn like our fingernails. It grows down from the coronet or coronary band in tubules and, when healthy, is tough and resilient rather than hard and rigid. The back part of the hoof comprises the sensitive (non-horny) heel.

The ground surface of the unshod hoof can be seen to have an outer rim of horn, the bottom or bearing surface of the wall which in a freshly trimmed foot, has an inner ring of whitish horn (the 'white line') and then a slightly arching sole of thinner, less tough horn. Extending forward from the heels is the triangular frog, which has evolved from the foot pad behind the toes of early ancestors, rather like a dog's paw. This is made of thick horn of india-rubber consistency. At the heels, the bearing surface of the wall turns inwards and runs alongside the frog, leaving grooves (the lacunae) between them. The turned-in wall is termed the bars; these peter out towards the point or apex of the frog. In the middle of the frog is an indentation called the cleft of the frog.

Inside the foot are three bones – the crescent-shaped pedal bone (called the first phalanx) which gives the foot its shape, the short pastern bone (second phalanx) which is partly inside the foot and partly outside, forming the bottom of the pastern, and the navicular bone, the small bone behind the pedal bone which forms a joint with it and the short pastern bone. This forms a pulley over which the deep digital flexor tendon runs (to lessen friction on it) before it attaches to the underside of the pedal bone.

There is a sensitive sole inside the foot above the horny one, and a sensitive frog, the back of the foot being taken up by a cartilagenous, fibrous wadge of tissue called the plantar or digital cushion. This, along with the frog, is one of the main means by which the foot absorbs and dissipates concussion and is, significantly, sited at the back of the foot because in fast gaits the heels impact with the ground first, and the heels are the part of the foot which expand most to help in this action. Nails are rarely put in the rear part of the shoe, so as not to hamper this expansion.

The surface of the pedal bone is covered by highly sensitive, blood-filled leaves of tissue known as the sensitive laminae, which interlock with the horny or insensitive laminae on the inside of the horny wall. There are additional projections from the laminae which also interlock, making an extremely strong bond to support the weight of the horse inside his horny hooves. So it could be said that the horse does not actually stand on the ground as we and many other animals do, but is supported or slung inside his feet by the laminae. A discussion of laminitis is out of place in this book, but I hope this description of the structure of the foot and the laminae will underline how devastating a disease it can be. When the bond between the laminae breaks down due to disturbance of the blood supply, the whole function and integrity of the foot is disturbed, sometimes irretrievably, although modern veterinary advances now save

many animals who would previously have been put down.

Continuing upwards from the ends of the pedal bone, and flanking the digital cushion, are two shields of cartilage called the lateral cartilages which can just be felt above the coronet at the heels. These sometimes ossify as a result of concussion, mainly in driving horses, especially the heavy types used for heavy haulage.

The foot is very well supplied with blood and nerves, and there are tendon and ligament attachments inside it, making it a miracle of animal design which should receive much more respect and attention than it often does.

Foot function is another of those areas which is subject to veterinary research and our knowledge of it is increasing all the time. The current idea is that as the foot hits the ground and takes the weight of the horse, it expands slightly, especially at the heels and lateral cartilages, the arched sole flattens down a little, the digital cushion is compressed and the insensitive frog is pressed against the ground. This squeezing action forces blood out of the blood vessels and capillaries (extremely fine vessels) in the sensitive tissues of the foot and up the leg. Valves in the veins prevent its return. When weight is removed as the foot is lifted, the vessels can expand again and are filled by fresh blood. In this way, oxygen and nutrients are constantly supplied to the foot and waste products removed.

Some researchers, however, feel that the sideways expansion of the heels and lateral cartilages may create a sucking action, drawing blood from beneath the pedal bone into and through tiny blood capillaries in the lateral cartilages, so spreading concussion rather like a gel saddle pad or, as one team described it, 'like a fluid-filled running shoe'. This idea certainly seems to make sense, the more so when one considers that at fast gaits the heels usually hit the ground first, receiving all the impact for a fraction of a second.

What everyone seems to agree upon is that the foot must land laterally evenly in order to distribute forces equally evenly up the leg, otherwise the soft and bony tissues of the limb will be subjected to stronger crushing forces in some parts and stretching forces in others than it was intended to bear.

Because the horse's only contact with the ground during action is via his feet (we hope), it is clear that healthy, strong and *comfortable* feet are vital to his ability and willingness to work well. A well-conformed, straight-moving horse will move his legs forward and back in a single plane of swing, landing his feet flat, except at speed when the heels hit the ground a fraction of a second before the rest of the bearing surface.

A farrier can tell from studying the wear patterns of the horse's shoes, or from unshod feet, how he lands his feet before he even sees him move. Because many horses do not move or land their feet straight, a great deal of expert judgement is needed to decide how much to try to alter the feet in order to attain even contact. All horses are different and it may not be wise to try to make their feet and action conform to 'proper' standards. Over-correcting the natural foot conformation of a mature horse with 'set' bones can disturb his normal force distribution to the extent that he is caused pain. However, if a horse's feet are misshapen and his action is crooked because of poor farriery, an expert farrier can gradually restore them to their previous, good conformation.

The basic guidelines to good foot balance are the same for any breed or type of horse, although some, such as heavy draught breeds, usually have flatter, larger feet with lower soles than riding breeds. Thoroughbreds are notorious for often having shallow feet, shelly horn, naturally low heels and flattish soles, but I hasten to add that many do have excellent feet.

The front feet bear more weight than the hind and are more circular in shape, the hind being more oval from toe to heel. Horses' feet are measured by placing a ruler across the widest part across the ground surface, then measuring again from the point where the wall turns in to form the bar to the centre of the toe. In a well-conformed front foot, those measurements should be the same. In the hindfeet, the latter measurement will be slightly longer because of the more oval shape.

In the front foot, if the measurement from toe to heel is significantly longer than that across the quarters, the toe of the foot is probably too long, unless the horn is broken and therefore out of shape; this condition often goes with heels which are too low. A foot this shape, particularly if it has been made so by poor farriery rather than being normal for the horse, is prone to uneven, excessive stresses which can impair the blood supply and lead to laminitis and navicular disease. The abnormal pressures impair the blood supply and the navicular bone comes under more pressure than in a better-conformed foot because there is more tendon pressure on it. Corns and extra strain on tendons and ligaments can also result.

Farriery practices which lead to this condition, which is fairly common, include: trimming too much off the heels where the horn is easier to trim and leaving too much at the toe which is harder and tougher; fitting shoes which do not go right back to the heels or very slightly beyond them ('short shoeing'); and leaving too long a time between trimming and shoeing.

A properly balanced foot should conform to certain criteria. When looking at front feet from in front, you should be able to imagine a straight line dropping right down the centre of a horse's leg and foot, ending at the toe; from behind the line should bisect the heels. In the hindfeet, the same line is often aimed for but in practice the horse family has a tendency to very slightly turned-in hocks and correspondingly turned out feet, so this natural feature must be allowed for. The important thing is that the feet land correctly and that the hind cannons are vertical and parallel. If the cannons are closer together at the top than the bottom, the horse is actually cow-hocked, which is a conformational weakness and a notable defect for horses which need hind-leg power such as jumpers and sprinters. We have imposed our man-made standards on hindfeet and legs for generations and it is commonly said that the imaginary line mentioned above must also bisect the heels of the back feet, when viewed from behind, and that the feet must face exactly forwards. This is not good or natural conformation, however, and horses so structured often experience extra stresses

a)

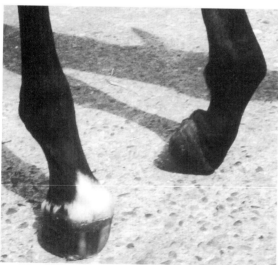

b)

a) and b) Deformed forelegs and feet, so-called 'contracted tendons', are caused by an unbalanced diet and the tendons being unable to keep up in terms of growth with the bones. They can be corrected with a balanced diet and expert veterinary attention and farriery

down the outsides of their hindlegs and feet.

Whether assessing the front or back feet, both sides of the coronet should be the same height from the ground when viewed from the front, and the slope of the outer (lateral) quarter can be very slightly more than the inner (medial) quarter which is usually naturally a little more upright. There should be no caving in of the hoof walls, outward bulges or flaring out at the ground surface. The ends of the coronets should also be the same height when viewed from the back. From the side, imagine another line passing down the centre of the pastern: this should reach the ground halfway along the foot. The front wall of the foot and the back wall of the heel should both be parallel to that line. The angle of the pastern/foot axis with the ground should be about 45° in the front feet and about 50° in the hindfeet. If you fail to see this straight-line pastern/hoof conformation, the horse's foot is not correctly balanced. If it appears to sag down at the coronet ('broken backward') or the line running down the pastern reaches the ground too far back, the toe is probably too long and the heels too low. If the coronet bulges upward ('broken forward') and the line reaches the ground too far forward, the toe is too short and the heels too high. The foot could be 'boxy' and upright or the heels contracted.

The straight pastern/hoof line is important because it affects the functioning of the fetlock which acts as a shock absorber for the horse. As the fetlock joint rotates forward and backward as the horse moves, the joints below it must also rotate somewhat in the same way, some more than others, rather like a series of hinges: however, if the line is broken in either direction, this action will be uneven and the function will not be so effective.

Looking at a foot from underneath, the two sides should be equal; you can use a ruler to check this, as when measuring the feet for size. Imagine a straight line running from toe to heel and on through the fetlock and up the back of the cannon; this should divide the foot and leg perfectly evenly, cutting the frog in two down its cleft and passing through the ergot on the point of the fetlock.

A simple test of whether the front feet and legs are straight is to flex the knee and bring the hoof up to the elbow or forearm. If the heels touch inward of the forearm or to the outside of it, you will know whether the horse in action will carry his forefeet too far inward or too far outward ('toeing in' or 'toeing out'). A horse approaching you should appear to have only two legs – his forelegs! They should be dead straight from top to bottom, not slanting inward or outward and his toes should be pointed directly forward. The hindlegs should follow the same plane exactly, which is why you will barely see them. A horse who toes in will move his feet out and then in on landing, and vice versa with a horse who toes out.

All these are simple, basic checks anyone can make and will give a good idea of good foot conformation and placement. As I have said, it is more important that the feet are placed down in the correct place and in the right way than that they get there via a straight plane, although the latter is certainly highly desirable. An expert farrier's advice should be taken about whether or not it is wise to try to interfere with a horse's action; sometimes it causes extra problems. The questions to ask are:

- Does the horse go sound, level, willingly and freely?
- Does he hit himself?

If the answers are 'yes' and 'no' respectively perhaps he is best left as he is. If you are still unsure, or if the horse often seems slightly lame or pottery or goes 'feeling' (sore), you should certainly discuss matters with your vet or farrier. Horses with poor foot conformation and action may well be able to be used for light hacking and pleasure work, but any horse with deviant action and poor foot (and leg) conformation will be at risk of interfering and even of bringing himself down. In showing and dressage, he will be marked down in most cases and may, in any sport, be unable to withstand the stress of hard work of any kind.

A recent development in farriery is the 'natural' or 'Four-point' trim which came about through research work done on American mustangs, involving studying the natural wear patterns of their feet. This trim mimicked the way these horses, with their tough, thick-soled feet, coped with the hard, abrasive ground surface of their natural habitat.

The natural wear pattern basically involves the hoof wearing itself squarish at the toe as the hoof 'breaks over' or turns over on the ground as the foreleg leaves the ground, and also wearing away at both the inner and outer quarters as the horse turns. This leaves the horse with an undeniably uneven bearing surface, something which is taboo in traditional farriery as it has always been felt that even pressure on the bearing surface means even stresses on the foot and leg. The horse was left with four points (which came to be known as 'pillars') of contact with the ground, especially on very hard ground.

For a few years now, some farriers have been simulating this natural wear by trimming horses' feet in a similar way, although it has been

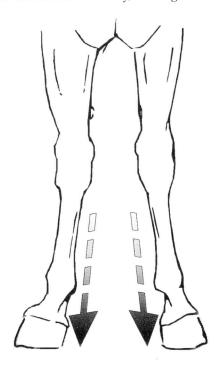

Apart from a 'broken forwards' conformation of the foot and pastern angle, these legs and feet are standing base wide and toeing out, exerting stretching forces on the soft tissues down the insides of the legs and excess pressure on the inside quarters of the feet

found to work best on horses with tough horn and thick soles. It is felt that this foot shape, which looks rather rectangular compared with the traditional, well-rounded-off version we are all used to, minimises muscular effort as the horse can break over his feet more quickly and with less effort (which also results in extra agility). The wearing or trimming away of the quarters so that they do not touch the ground on the bearing surface is believed to prevent the wall flaring out at the sides and actually strengthen the heels, so reducing stress on the tendons and ligaments.

Thirty-six years ago, I bought a young horse with a very short back (which at the time I thought was a good conformation point). He often over-reached (a common fault with youngsters and particularly with short-backed horses) and my farrier squared off the foot at the toe, as this was the way the horse naturally wore his feet; the farrier also set his shoes back slightly, rolling the toes as well. This greatly improved the over-reaching and by the time the horse was five years old, more muscled up and working well, the fault stopped entirely. He continued to be shod that way for many years afterwards, however, and that farrier, all that time ago, accepted that the normal rounded-off hooves we regard as correct are not a natural shape for horses' feet. He did not trim the quarters away, but he did improve the way of going of most of the horses he shod.

Like all new ideas, the natural or Four-point trim is controversial but it certainly suits a lot of horses. It is, however, apparently difficult actually to shoe a horse to match the trim, although new shoes and shoeing systems are appearing which try to accommodate this natural foot conformation. One argument against this trim is that this may be the way American mustangs wear their feet but it does not do for all horses. It nevertheless certainly suited my young horse and I believe would have suited many horses I have known since, plus an old Thoroughbred mare I had until recently who had arthritic hind fetlocks – but my current farrier would not trim her that way! It will be interesting to watch developments in this field.

Backs

There is probably no one part of the horse which is the subject of more controversy than the back. When even veterinary surgeons argued for years among themselves about whether or not the back can bend or flex, either up and down or from side to side, what hope does this leave the rest of us? I have in my library (which is nowhere near as grand as that sounds) two articles written in the 1970s by eminent veterinary surgeons, one claiming that the horse's back is almost rigid and any apparent flexion is an optical illusion, the other that it is quite flexible, if obviously not as flexible as that of a cat or dog, and that if it were not the horse would be incapable of performing the athletic feats for which he is renowned.

In *Equi*, a magazine I published in the 1980s, a most eminent riding teacher maintained that the back was fairly inflexible and that the optical illusion of 'bend' was accomplished by the muscles between the ribs contracting and bringing one side of the ribcage together whilst stretching the other. Also in *Equi*, a famous dressage trainer, author and rider presented a very thorough treatment, with photographic evidence of live horses' spines bending this way and that and dissected vertebral columns doing the same. These were photographs of horses and riders taken from above, using a special scaffold, and he presented a learned and reasonable argument. However, some years after his death it was pronounced to be rubbish by a senior research fellow in Physiology at a British university. Confusion, confusion!

Today, owing to research and modern radiographic techniques, we know that the back is, collectively, slightly flexible, although more so in some areas than others. By 'collectively', I mean that there is a little movement between most of the vertebrae which, together, adds up to enough for the horse's purposes but certainly not enough to enable his spine to flex evenly along the line of a circle or to bend in an arc over fences, as is so often shown in equitation manuals. It has been said often enough that the horse's spine was never evolved to carry weight on top in addition to bearing the natural downward force of his heavy chest and abdominal contents, which are slung by strong membranes from underneath it.

Most of the vertebrae of the spine move against their neighbours to some variable extent according to their places in the line. The neck and tail parts of the spine are obviously the most flexible; in between them, it is much less flexible. The crucial lumbo-sacral joint enables the hindquarters to engage up and down and is largely responsible for the ability of the hips to 'swing' from side to side, although the spine also flexes laterally slightly, particularly in the slower gaits. In canter, the lumbo-sacral joint is where most of the lateral and vertical movement takes place. At the gallop, the spine is held almost rigid by the large and strong back muscles as a protective mechanism to maintain stability in order to prevent over-flexion and injury. When jumping, also, the horse must maintain a stiff, straight (not rounded) back in order for the tremendous force produced by his hindlegs and quarters to be transmitted along it and propel his body over an obstacle. Finally, the five fused vertebrae of the croup or sacrum clearly make this area rigid.

There are three normal sorts of joint between vertebrae:

- Those which occur between the bodies or lower parts of each vertebra (below the neural canal which forms the tunnel for the spinal cord) consist of a slight convexity on the surface of one bony arch which fits into a corresponding concavity on the arch of its neighbour. There is a disc of cartilage between them and the whole little joint is bound together and protected by ligaments and a bursa or joint capsule.
- The part above the neural canal is called the arch and the arches of neighbouring vertebrae also touch or articulate and have ligamentous 'bindings' which are more elastic than ligaments elsewhere in the body, a feature which enhances the spine's flexibility.
- The transverse processes (side projections) of the fourth, fifth and sixth lumbar vertebrae also articulate, as do those of the sixth lumbar and first sacral vertebrae.

These joints are normal, but sometimes, due to extreme athletic effort, flexion is overdone, and processes which should never touch do so. There may be contact between other lumbar transverse processes (pinching and tearing the soft tissues between them and obviously causing great pain), and a contact which is commonly known as 'kissing spines' is that between the tops of dorsal processes. When abnormal contact is made, the bone itself, as well as the associated soft tissues, can be bruised or even fractured and, when healing takes place, the processes can become ankylosed or fused together, reducing flexibility. Although this must be very painful whilst it is going on, many horses do not exhibit actual lameness although they may well show the normal signs of a painful back; once the fusion is complete, there is probably no pain, although there must be some mechanical stiffness.

The normal vertebral joints can also become ankylosed if they are sufficiently stressed and injured and, as nerves pass out from the spinal cord through matching grooves on the edges of neighbouring vertebrae, nerve damage and resulting paralysis can occur. The major injury of a broken back, which is usually caused by falling, will also obviously cause severe paralysis. Sometimes, however, vertebrae can be fractured in such a way that nerve damage does not occur, although there is still pain.

Jumping horses and racehorses, whose spines are pushed to their limits, show most clinical back problems but there must be many, many more horses and ponies who are branded 'difficult', 'a rogue', 'cold backed', 'uncooperative' or downright 'unrideable' who are, in fact, reacting to the pain of work and are telling their human partners this in the only way they can. Chronic lameness can also be a result of a back problem, often from compensatory action.

It is not only bony injuries which cause pain, of course; soft tissue injuries, normally tears of muscle, tendon, ligament and connective tissues, cause considerable pain, as most of us know from personal experience. Sometimes, when the pain becomes slight but constant (chronic) the horse simply bears it stoically but never works really well, causing distress and frustration for him and annoyance and disappointment for his rider.

In my practical experience, poor riding technique is one of the most common causes of back problems, rather than simply the work the horse does, although a lack of understanding of correct saddling is certainly an equally important factor. Riders who do not absorb the natural movements of their horse's back with their spines, pelvises and hips tend to block the horse's movement and he then often braces himself against the discomfort. Banging up and down on the back is obviously going to cause discomfort and create a force against which the horse will defend himself by tensing and stiffening up, sometimes to the extent of over-stressing his various soft tissues and, if the situation is bad enough, injuring his vertebrae as well if he is in active work. The combined effects of poor riding and bad saddle fit can easily be imagined.

A common type of injury or disorder in any horse showing a back problem is that the muscles of the back go into spasm, which can be really painful. As well as the muscle tissue itself being painful, there is a constant pull on the associated tendon tissue. The spasm may be on only one side of the back, making it look uneven, or, perhaps more unusually, on both sides. Physical therapies of various sorts aim to release this spasm rather than to 'replace' vertebrae, which may not in fact be displaced.

In driving horses, consideration of the horse's movements is also important, and whilst they do not carry weight, overloading their vehicles is a frequent cause of hindquarter and back strain, as is pulling them through heavy going or against an obstacle such as a boulder in the ground.

Tack and harness

Horses also adopt faulty, unnatural postures to avoid the discomfort and pain caused by badly fitted and incorrectly adjusted tack and harness. Tight bearing reins, still used in some harness sports including racing and some forms of private driving, deny the horse free use of his head and neck so that he cannot use them to balance

Side reins have to be very carefully adjusted if they are to be not only useful but also not damaging. If loose, as here, they do no more than give the horse a suggestion of a slight weight on the bit which may be all the trainer wants. If adjusted so as to provide a noticeable contact when the horse is standing naturally, they will actually prevent a horse going 'long and low', if this is what is wanted, by preventing him stretching his nose out and down: instead he will be forced to become overbent. Side reins are, however, very often adjusted tighter than that and actually cause significant tension and stressful compensatory movement in the muscles of the neck, shoulders, back and quarters, encouraging the horse to produce an incorrect flexion, a kink in the neck in front of the withers, a lowered back and trailing hindquarters and legs – all of which are exactly what a good trainer does not want.

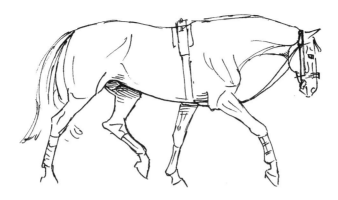

The chambon is a useful schooling aid which, correctly adjusted, simply encourages the horse to go with his head down (not overbent) and his topline rounded. It has no direct influence on the hindquarters but horses usually respond by also raising their backs and bellies and lowering their hindquarters which is exactly the effect required for correct muscle and 'outline' development

his body as he needs to do to push forward into his collar; this causes a great deal of unnatural muscle stiffness of the neck, back, loins and hindquarters in particular, with consequent back injury, discomfort and pain. Riding horses, particularly in showing and the competitive sports of dressage and, to a lesser extent, showjumping, often have to work under the handicap of a restricted head and neck. There is still a common misconception that holding the head and neck up and in by means of the reins or training aids, particularly of the 'outline-fixing' variety such as tight side-reins, draw-reins and running reins, will produce a shape (outline or 'frame') of the head and neck which looks as though the horse is 'on the bit', in hand or even collected. In reality, the horse will very often become heavy in hand or persistently go behind the bit or else appear to be going sweetly but actually be avoiding working and be holding and using his body in injurious ways to get round the lack of freedom of his head and neck. This places unnatural stresses on his body, which can only result in discomfort and pain.

Apart from the inhumanity of forcing horses to work in ways which cause them distress, discomfort or pain, there is the practical consideration of how it affects their work. As I have said, horses who find normal movement uncomfortable, painful or impossible will adopt unnatural, compensatory ways of moving which may be quite inappropriate for their jobs. For instance, a dressage horse whose neck and back have been made so stiff or muscle-bound due to incorrect techniques that he cannot work properly cannot be expected to have a willing attitude to his work, one which will produce that all-important sparkle and 'oomph' sought after in dressage today, and a showjumper whose legs and back are constantly uncomfortable due to the way he is ridden and trained similarly cannot be expected to cope with his fences and clear them, which is the whole point of this sport.

Apart from buying horses which are suitably conformed for the job the purchaser has in mind, it is also essential, for optimal performance, for them to be trained correctly.

CHAPTER

5

SHAPING UP TO THE JOB

We know that horses and ponies come in all sorts of shapes and sizes. Even people who are not particularly interested in horses know what type of horse is likely to win the Epsom Derby and what type is likely to be seen pulling a plough or a brewery dray. Between these two extremes, however, certainly in the middle range, even experienced horse people cannot always tell exactly what sort of job a horse will be suitable for. The truth is that most mid-range horses of good basic conformation can perform any job creditably well. 'Ride-and-drive' animals are rarer these days, not because the type does not exist but because there seems to be a scarcity of people able to train and produce them, driving not being as widespread as it used to be.

The first thing to look for in any animal is individual balance and symmetry. You could take two well-conformed horses yet if you imagined the forehand of one attached to the hindquarters of the other, you would end up with a horse completely out of synchrony with himself. Developing an eye for overall synchrony (as well as the details of individual parts, which is mainly dealt with in Chapter 6) is best done by attending as many high-level shows or competitions as you can and just looking at the winners, letting their shape and balance – both standing still and in motion – soak into your mind and become part of your inner feel and knowledge. This is the essential starting point before you begin to assess the individual parts.

As you become accustomed to just letting a

horse 'fill your eye' as the saying goes, it is a good plan to stand back from him with an open mind, not expecting anything; just let your eyes run over his body and see where they come to rest. Very often, the part where they linger will be where there is something wrong, some fault which is spoiling the whole picture, even if you cannot immediately put your finger on it. (As a practitioner of shiatsu for horses, I find that this is also a good way of initially seeing where there seems to be some sort of indication of pain, discomfort or difficulty. Invariably, this assessment turns out to be accurate even though the horse may not be standing awkwardly or unevenly, or even looking out of sorts.)

A basic blueprint

It is logical to start in the middle range of horse type and assess the look and proportions of a generally good all-round horse. There are many theories about joint angles, proportions and diagrammatic systems for assessing conformation, some quite complicated and others very simple. The following is one of the simplest.

You can best assess the precise conformation balance of a stationary horse by marking off certain proportions and measurements on a photograph. First, do make sure that he is standing properly for the photo, to attention and ideally *not* in the traditional photo pose, with the pair of legs furthest away from the camera slightly under the horse, so that they separate from the pair nearest the camera from knees and hocks down. Try to get the horse standing square and straight with his forelegs perpendicular and in the same plane (no leaning forward or back – if he cannot naturally stand straight he is not suitable for athletic work, anyway) and his hindlegs also in the same plane, so that from the side and in the photo he looks as though he only has two legs, one of each. This is not essential but it prevents any uncertainties of measurement. He should look as though he is standing naturally and not be uncomfortable or off balance.

Ignore the current fashion in showing some breeds and types in hand (in the U.S.A. at halter), where the horse stands with his head high, his back hollow and his legs stretched out forward and backward, particularly backward. This presentation makes it extremely difficult to judge his true conformation (which may be why it is so popular in the show ring!) and also encourages stress and strain on the back, exactly what you *do not* want in a riding horse. It is certainly useless for our purposes here.

When taking the photograph, make sure that the bottom of the frame and the two feet nearest the camera are perfectly horizontal and parallel, to avoid any untrue or misleading perspectives in the final picture. You must be absolutely sideways on to the horse so that an imaginary beam

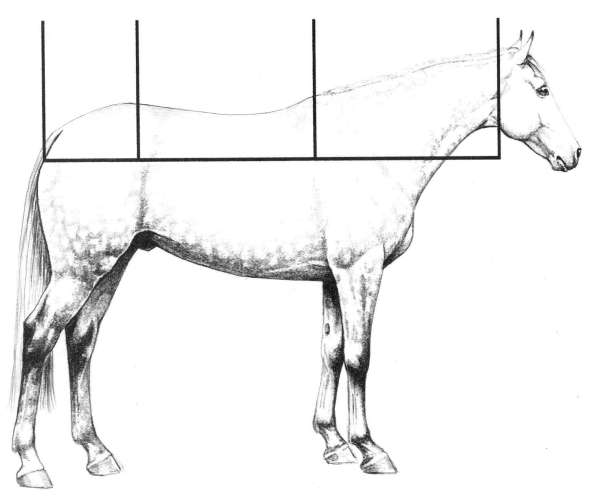

A starting point. The section on the left should be about half the size of the two on the right for basic symmetry

Shallow depth of girth. Such horses may not be good for stamina-type sports as they may not have the heart and lung room for really good respiration and exchange of carbon dioxide for oxygen in the lungs, on which depends the ability to work. The author has known several exceptions to this rule, however

going from the camera lens to his side would form a right angle to the horse and be parallel to the ground – which is why good equestrian photographers need flexible, strong knees or the ability to stand easily on tiptoe! The beam must be pointed directly at the horse's centre of gravity which is, for our purposes, about two-thirds of the way down his ribcage and about 6 inches (15 cm) back from the elbow.

On the resulting photograph, first draw in the ground line with a ruler and black pen. Now draw a line at right angles to the ground line up through the horse's poll, another one up through the highest point of his withers and two more at the point of the croup and the root of the tail. Draw another line horizontal with the ground line immediately underneath and touching the breastbone at the girth, running through the other lines, and a final horizontal line immediately above the horse's head, similarly cutting through the vertical lines.

Now you have a number of squares and rectangles on the photograph. Take the ruler and note down the following measurements: from the poll to the withers along the horizontal line, from the withers to the croup and from the croup to the root of the tail. Next, measure

vertically from the withers to the breastbone and from the breastbone to the ground. The measurements from the poll to the withers and the withers to the croup should be about equal and from the croup to the root of the tail should be about half as far. The measurement from the withers to the breastbone should be no less than that from the breastbone to the ground and ideally a little more. In fact, with the exception of the one from the croup to the tail, all the measurements should be very nearly identical, with the croup-to-tail distance no less than half as far.

These guidelines come up with a good basic result – either the horse has good symmetry and general proportions and should have a good natural balance or he does not. You must, however, allow for horses with exceptionally high or low withers when considering the vertical measurements. But the actual slope of the quarter from the croup to the root of the tail does not matter too much; it is the distance which is the important thing.

Horses used for different disciplines are often different shapes within these basic measurements – for instance, a sloping croup is often taken to indicate jumping ability if it stems from a generous bone formation to allow ample and secure muscle attachment. However, the horse should not normally be croup high, where the croup is higher than the withers. (Youngstock are an exception to this, and also many sprinters and 'power' jumpers.) Draw another horizontal line from the withers to the croup and see whether or not it is parallel with the ground line. A horse which is croup high according to this criterion will always have problems with his saddle, which will tend to ride forward and dig in behind his shoulders and just below the withers. If he is used under saddle for only short periods such as sprinting (many sprinters are croup high), or if he is a harness horse, this may not matter, but you certainly would not want a dressage horse, a pleasure horse or hack, a hunter or an endurance horse with this conformation. Remember, though, what I said earlier about the true horizontal balance of the horse taken from the shoulder blade fulcrum to the hip joint; this is something to which we shall return.

General pointers

The top line

The neck should arch attractively down and back from the poll, joining the withers smoothly with no dip in front, except possibly in a horse in poor condition. The withers themselves should not be too high or 'sharp' but well defined, and should flow smoothly into a level back which rises, again smoothly, to broad, short loins which themselves rise to the croup, after which there is a dip towards the root of the tail. The whole appearance of this, the horse's top line, should be a series of smooth curves rather than angles.

The forehand

The front or forehand of a horse is important because it affects the horse's ability to absorb jar during movement and therefore the comfort of his ride, and has some influence on whether or not the rider feels safe in that she has 'plenty in

Just for fun, see how many conformational faults you can find on this horse. The answers are given on page 91

front of her'. Another expression for this is that the horse has 'a good length of rein' or 'a good front'. For a good slope of shoulder, the point of the elbow should lie in front of a vertical line dropped from the front of the withers. The chestnut on the inside of the foreleg should be level with or slightly above the point of the hock of the hindleg on the same side, and the angle of the shoulder (taken along the bony ridge or spine of the shoulder blade from the point of the shoulder running up to the withers) should be about 40°–45° in a riding horse. The angle of the hoof wall with the ground at the toe and the long pastern bone of the foreleg should,

according to traditional wisdom, show an identical angle, although some researchers into conformation and function say that this is not important so long as the hoof/pastern axis is straight and somewhere between the two measurements given. (In the hindleg, a slightly more upright angle is normal, say about 50° or even 55°.)

It is helpful if you can fit at least two to four fingers' width between the horse's elbow and his ribcage to allow for a free swing of the foreleg forward and backward and thus the longest possible stride. If the elbow joint is 'tied in' to the ribcage by skin and the joint is not 'open' as described, the horse will be unable to extend his foreleg fully in front, no matter how free his actual shoulder movement.

As for the head, you should be able to fit your fist between the two round lower jawbones at the throat so that there is ample room for the windpipe and so for free air passage. The angle at the throat should not be sharp and cramped but have a rounded arch shape so that the horse does not kink his airways when flexing his poll and jaw. You should also be able to fit two fingers' width between the wing of the atlas (the first vertebra of the neck which forms the joint with the skull) and the top of the lower jawbone, just below the base of the ear. Measured from the poll to the top lip, the head should not be longer than the measurement taken from just behind the horse's ears to the point where the neck joins the withers. Because the horse's head and neck act as his natural balancing pole, like a human's arms, a big heavy head, particularly on a long neck, makes the horse clumsy, inclined to go 'into the ground', heavy in hand and with a tendency to go too much 'on his forehand' naturally. Too small a head with too short a neck may mean he cannot balance himself very well; he may not be very agile and could find it difficult to recover from falls and pecks.

The way the neck comes out of the shoulders or is set on to them is also important. Seen from the side, if the neck appears to be low-set so that the horse seems to have hardly any chest below the base of his neck, particularly if the neck angle veers towards the horizontal and,

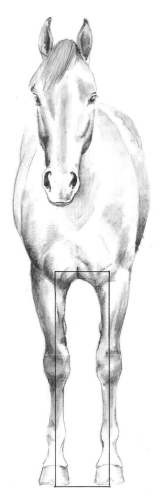

From the front, the forelegs should appear like two straight columns with a straight line equally bisecting them

even worse, has a large, heavy head on the end of it, the horse will always be boring into the ground and be almost impossible to school into a light-in-hand, well-balanced ride. The head and neck are crucial to the horse's ability to distribute his weight favourably in action, particularly when negotiating rough country and obstacles.

From the front, the forelegs should appear like two straight columns. A straight line dropped from the point of the shoulder should pass down the exact centre of the knee, cannon, fetlock and foot to the toe. A reasonable guide is that you should be able to fit another hoof between the two feet; if you can do so, and the legs are straight and not slanted in or out, the horse will have a good chest width, neither too wide nor too narrow. Also look from the front at the slope from bottom (points) to top (wither area) of the horse's shoulder blades. They should obviously be closer together at their tops than at their points (from which the legs run straight down). If the shoulder blades are quite wide apart at the wither area, this will produce a rolling, side-to-side action which is most uncomfortable to sit on but of no consequence in a heavy draught horse where this conformation is common. Shoulder blades which are wide apart at the top combined with flattish withers and lots of flesh or muscle are called 'loaded shoulders'. Some Cleveland Bay and Irish Draught horses have this structure as both breeds began life as pack and draught breeds respectively, but any breed with cold blood in its ancestry, including today's popular continental competition warmbloods, can throw up this fault for riding work. It is also a conformation point of some cobs and chunkier ponies.

From the side, the forelegs should be straight, with the horse neither appearing to lean forward over them nor seeming to be standing back on his heels. Drop an imaginary straight line vertically from the centre of the shoulder to the ground; it should go straight down the middle of the leg to the fetlock joint and then make contact with the ground just behind the heel.

The hindquarters

From the back, assuming that the horse is not thin or poorly muscled up, the thighs just

behind the stifles should be the same width as the hips above them and the thigh muscles should meet between the legs. The second thighs, too, should meet this standard and the stifles, like the elbows, should be open for a scopey stride. They should turn very slightly outwards like the hindfeet and the cannons should be vertical to the ground, not sloped inward nor bowed outward. Again, a good guide is that you should be able to fit the width of another hoof between the two hindfeet. Horses with 'dead straight' hocks and hindfeet, as described earlier, often go rather 'wide behind' once in motion; this stresses the whole hindleg, particularly down the outside, and is an uncomfortable action to sit on.

Seen from behind, the hindquarters of a normally muscled-up horse should fill a square, with the croup as the highest point, the hips and thighs the same width and the bottom of the

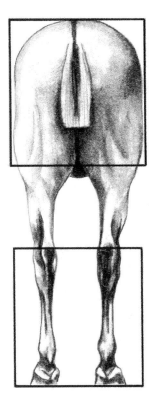

You should be able to use two identically-sized squares to gauge the conformation and balance of a horse's hindquarters, like this, and as described in the text

square drawn along between the thighs. The same sized square can be used for the hind cannons; the distance from the points of the hocks to the ground should be the same height as the first square.

From the side, the hindlegs should be set neither too far under the horse nor too far behind. You should be able to drop an imaginary line from the point of the buttock, down touching the point of the hock and straight down the back of the cannon and fetlock to the ground. The stifle should be directly under the highest point of the croup. Too far forward and it could indicate a 'straight' hindleg with insufficient leverage for thrust; too far back and it could indicate an 'overbent' leg which is too weak to work well.

Symmetry

A major point regarding overall symmetry and balance is that the two halves of the horse, left and right, should match and look like mirror images of each other. In real life, most horses have some very minor asymmetry which may not even be noticed. Most horses also prefer going on one rein to the other and may even be permanently slightly curved in that direction, and some are asymmetrical or twisted for all sorts of other reasons: bad conformation, injuries from strenuous work, kicking their stables or usually from falls (not necessarily during work), struggling to get up or even poor farriery.

To judge a horse for symmetry of his left and right halves, you must study both left and right sides and also study him from the front and from the back. The back view will give you a lot of information if you can stand behind and slightly above him, say on a crate, bucket or fence rail. If you look at a horse from the front and back and he seems at all lopsided, unbalanced, twisted from poll to tail anywhere, under-developed on one side or over-developed on the other, leaning to or curved in one direction even when standing supposedly straight – or anything which indicates that he does not have two virtually equal sides – get your vet to examine him if he is yours or to give an opinion on him if you are having him vetted for purchase. 'One-sided' horses, and they are many, can almost always be improved

by correct schooling work and some kind of physical therapy.

Other conformational faults should be symmetrical so that the horse can at least cope evenly with them. For instance, if the horse is very slightly knock-kneed, check whether one or both knees bends in; both bending in just a little is a less serious fault than just one. If one point of shoulder or one hock or hip is higher than the other, it could be quite a significant fault once the horse goes into action. (A vet, farrier or physiotherapist may well come up with reasons and treatments for these kinds of faults.) Asymmetry decreases the efficiency of the horse's action and his energy expenditure and distribution in motion. It also places equally asymmetrical stresses on the body which, as we have seen, so often result in injuries, particularly when borne over a long period of time. The horse may go lame gradually or suddenly and you may have no idea why – he may not have had a fall or been cast or kicked. If this happens, it is probably due to the cumulative effects of uneven distribution of forces on his body.

A good way to appreciate the damaging and pain-inducing effects of asymmetry is to wear (at your own risk!) two shoes from a different pair with slightly different heel heights for a day, and see how uncomfortable you feel, even starting to feel some pain, at the end of a few hours.

Other proportional systems

Head length

The length of the horse's head, provided it is not over-large or tiny (which can only be assessed by looking at his overall balance), can be used as a base measurement for various other systems of judging proportion.

In a well-proportioned horse, the length of the head should roughly equal:

- the length of the neck
- the depth of the girth from withers to breastbone
- the length of the hindleg from the point of hock to the ground

- the distance from the chestnut on the inside of the foreleg to the ground
- the distance from the point of shoulder to the highest point of the withers
- the distance from the withers to the hip bone (although this may be a little longer in mares and a little shorter in very short-backed horses such as most Arabs and their crosses); you should be able to fit the width of your hand between the horse's last rib and the point of his hip for a 'well ribbed-up' barrel, which means the back should be long enough to allow the horse to be 'scopey' and yet short enough to make him nimble at the same time
- the distance from the point of the stifle to the highest point of the croup
- the distance from the point of the stifle to the point of the hock (ideally this should be a little longer)
- the distance from the point of shoulder to the point of elbow (actually a little shorter)

There should be two to two and a half head lengths fitting between the point of buttock and the point of shoulder, and about the same measurement should also be the horse's height at withers and croup. If you work all this out on your photograph, you will see that, pedantic though it may sound, it does work out in practice on a good horse and, of course, the measurements are all approximations.

Body square

Another guide to overall balance is to be able to fit the horse's body, seen from the side and excluding head and neck, into a square.

The three-thirds system

Again seen from the side, most of the horse's body is divided into thirds. The first is from just behind the poll, where it meets the first neck vertebra (the atlas), to just in front of the shoulder blade. The second is from just behind the shoulder blade to just in front of the point of hip. The final third goes from the latter spot to the point of buttock.

The hindquarter triangle

The distances from the point of the buttock to the point of the hip, the point of the buttock to the stifle and the stifle to the point of the hip should be the same, thus forming an equilateral triangle.

Leg bone proportions

Whilst on the subject of proportions, another interesting little item I found in my archives was a table from an obviously old magazine cutting giving the ratios of different bones in the horse's body. My accompanying notes said that the author meant the figures to be guidelines, not absolute requirements. I have no trace of the magazine it came from but I hope it will be of interest.

Table 1. Bone Ratios

Bones	Average	Range
Scapula/humerus	1.8/1	1.4–1.9/1
Humerus/radius	0.667/1	0.625–0.91/1
Radius-carpus/		
Carpus-metacarpus	1.5/1	1.3–1.8/1
Metacarpus/phalanges	1.4/1	1.1–1.6/1
Ilium/femur	1.0/1	0.97–1.3/1
Femur/tibia	1.0/1	1.0–1.3/1

Much is made of the length of horses' cannon bones and we know that they are always required to be 'short', but why is this? The terms 'short cannon bones' and 'well let down hocks' are examples of points of equine conformation which are particularly important when it comes to coping with the stresses of movement. There is not one job which horses are required to perform which demands long cannons!

The foreleg cannon bones should be significantly shorter than the forearms. Likewise, the horse's second thigh bone or gaskin, from stifle to hock, should look long in comparison to his hindleg cannon bone so that the hocks look 'well let down' or 'close to the ground'. This structure produces less stress on the tendons and ligaments in the lower legs where there are no muscles. The tendons, to recap, are continuations of the muscles in forearm and thigh and attach to the feet at various points so that when their respective muscles contract there is a pull on the tendon and the leg moves. The ligaments help to bind the bones together, supporting the skeleton.

Short cannon bones mean the tendons and ligaments in the lower leg are correspondingly short. A short structure is always stronger than a longer one of the same circumference, so short cannons are likely to stand up better to work. You can easily test this by taking a stick of a thickness you think you can break reasonably easily and breaking it in half just by holding it at its ends; then take one half again by the ends and try again to break it. You may well succeed but you will notice that it requires a lot more strength to break it the second time.

Short cannon bones in the hindlegs produce greater leverage to push the horse forward, or up if jumping. In fact, a long second thigh bone has been shown by scientific assessment (which will be discussed in more detail in Chapter 7) to be a significant element of jumping horses' conformation, particularly in the Puissance jumper who has to rely on muscle power and the leverage of his upper hindlegs rather than speed-produced impetus to carry him over fences.

'Bone' and weight

There is one question which seems to be particularly important to horse people and that is how much 'bone' a horse has. This means the measurement around his front cannon bones just below the knee. An old standard stipulated that you should only just be able to touch the tips of your middle finger and thumb when you put your hand around this area, but this is fairly meaningless because different people have fingers of different lengths. Measuring this spot with a tape measure is also fairly meaningless because the measurement will clearly be taking in the tendons and ligaments running down the

back of the leg, so you are clearly not getting a measurement of just bone at all.

Some people use 'bone' measurement to gauge how much weight a horse should be 'up to' (able to carry). It is said that a horse with 8 in or 20 cm of bone, such as the average 16 hand (163 cm) Thoroughbred, can carry up to 13 st, 182 lb or 82.5 kg, a horse with 9 in or 23 cm of bone should be able to carry up to 15 st, 210 lb or 95.25 kg and over that the horse is classed as a heavyweight hunter or riding horse. (Despite the E.U.'s efforts, the horse world of the U.K. and Ireland, as well as North America, still usually operates informally in Imperial measurements).

Although the above may be taken as a very rough guide to how much weight a horse can carry, which is obviously very important for an athletic performer, I feel it is rather on the harsh side. A better guide is to work on a horse's being able to carry up to a sixth of his own weight relatively easily, although ponies and cobs are generally accepted as being able to carry more, sometimes a good deal more, than this. You should in any case have a ready idea of your horse's weight so you could take him to your local weighbridge, where you should weigh him without his saddle and not stand on the platform yourself, or you could use the following tables.

To measure a horse's girth you can use a special weigh tape, which is often available from feed merchants or tack shops, or you can just use a piece of string. Pass it right round your horse's girth just behind the withers, keeping it vertical to the ground, and holding it just tight enough to press in his flesh slightly when he is breathing *out*. Then measure the length of the string, refer to the table for his weight and divide it by six to arrive at a reasonable weight for him to carry. The horse must be neither fat nor thin for this process – just so that you can feel his ribs easily but not actually see them.

There are other points of conformation which will be examined in Chapter 6, but I hope the above general guidelines on assessing a mid-range type of horse (between extreme strength/ heavy horse conformation and ultimate speed/ bloodhorse conformation) will prove of practical

Table 2. Ponies and Cobs

Girth in inches	40	42.5	45	47.5	50	52.5	55	57.5
Girth in cm	101	108	114	120	127	133	140	146
Bodyweight in lb	100	172	235	296	368	430	502	562
Bodyweight in kg	45	77	104	132	164	192	234	252

Table 3. Horses

Girth in inches	55	57.5	60	62.5	65	67.5	70	72.5	75	77.5	80	82.5
Girth in cm	140	146	152	159	165	171	178	184	190	199	203	206
Bodyweight in lb	538	613	688	776	851	926	1014	1090	1165	1278	1328	1369
Bodyweight in kg	240	274	307	346	380	414	453	486	520	570	593	611

(Tables based on work of Glushanok, Rochlitz & Skay, 1981)

help at a basic level when assessing conformation. It is particularly useful for prospective purchasers to ask vendors to send a photograph of their horse before travelling to see the animal. Then you can just take a photocopy of the photograph and measure it up without marking the original, which may have to be returned.

Shaping up

Let us now take a general look at the basic body shapes and types which should be best suited to different jobs. In Chapter 1, we said that skeletal structure was not the most important factor to consider and that muscle type and function and, most of all, the efficiency of the horse's nervous control of those muscles were the ultimate deciders of his *métier*. If you consistently look at and study the types of horses which are successful in the different equestrian sports, however, you will usually notice similarities of type, particularly in the higher echelons of the sports. Probably the easiest types to pick out are dressage horses and endurance horses. Event horses, too, are recognisable and of a very similar type to steeplechasers and point-to-pointers. Unfortunately for the student of equine conformation, showjumpers and hunters (not show hunters) are notorious for coming in all shapes

and sizes. In the U.K., we are barely familiar with sports such as cutting, reining, barrel racing and Quarter Horse racing but shall look at them briefly because it is useful to understand them. We shall also examine different types of racehorse (there is quite a difference between a sprinter and a stayer), polo ponies, harness racers, carriage horses and heavy horses. Show horses of various types are also significant and, in many cases, easily recognised. High School horses are best built in a specific way but it is clear from looking at old engravings and paintings that, at least in former centuries, all sorts of types were schooled in this specialised and difficult work; today, although this is still possible, High School horses, at least the types which perform the more difficult airs and certainly those above the ground, are of a recognisable type.

The most extreme and easily recognisable types of horses and ponies are usually to be found at the higher levels of any of the disciplines; lower down in the competitive field, most horses are quite capable of being all-rounders at a reasonable level.

Dressage horses
Because competitive dressage demands the conformation points required of any good riding horse, if to a more marked extent, we shall look in more depth at dressage horses than at those

required for other equestrian sports. This does not mean that other sports are less important or demanding, simply that it is important to recognise good riding conformation for any saddle horse.

Today more than ever the charismatic quality called presence is essential in the competitive dressage horse, plus a certain amount of size – horses over 17 hands high are quite the norm in the competitive dressage arena these days. The horse must present a smooth, flowing outline and preferably be handsome rather than flashy, pretty or beautiful, although there are always exceptions. (In the competitive arena, there is a loosely standardised type and horses have to meet judging criteria, which rather puts paid to the chances of a horse which does not have the appropriate conformation, size and movement. However, the Classical Riding Club, both in the U.K. and in its overseas branches, has ruled that horses be marked according to their natural type and action – a huge, fair and understanding step forward. There are also rider marks and other bonus marks, another sensible and encouraging innovation.)

A swinging, elastic, straight movement is essential with the ability both to collect and to extend, particularly in the higher echelons of the sport. Although a very great deal of improvement can be made in the horse's appearance by correct work and thus muscular development, this should be done with a view to improving the horse's natural attributes rather than attempting to turn a sow's ear into a silk purse, which can never be entirely successful. Although one can get away with various faults in an 'ordinary' riding horse, particularly if he is not required for showing or for hard work, competitive dressage, certainly at the higher levels, demands near-perfect make and shape, so one has to start with the right material. Naturally harmonious, symmetrical conformation, presence, confidence and free, straight movement with the natural inclination to flex but not to overflex the joints are what to look for in the first place. Uphill conformation (slightly 'wither-high') is also wanted.

Unfortunately, many dressage horses are incorrectly trained, often in outline-fixing devices,

and there is a concentration on forehand appearance, rather than hind-end thrust which should lead to the horse's finding his own balance and carriage in front as he needs to for co-operative, free movement. They thus appear to suffer from muscle hypertrophy and look stiff and muscle-bound, not to mention stressed out, all of which is wrong, to say the least.

The set of the neck and head are important in the dressage horse. In the higher levels of the sport the ability to collect and go in true self-carriage is essential. This will be easier to achieve if the horse has a natural set of the head and neck to facilitate it rather than having the neck set low on the shoulders and an angular or thick jowl which will make it uncomfortable and difficult for him to 'bridle', i.e. carry the front line of his face slightly (around 5°) in front of the vertical. Conversely, a 'swan neck', which kinks in its lower half in front of the withers and arches behind the ears, may produce a horse which goes with the front of his face positioned where it is wanted but his flexion will be false. He must learn to push up his neck from its base, from under the lower bend of the S-shape made by the vertebrae, and a swan-necked horse finds it more or less impossible to do this to the degree required for correct work. The work involved in trying, however, will improve him as a general riding horse.

The poll should be long and supple enough (and the throat open enough) to enable the horse to flex at the poll so that it is his highest point (disregarding his ears!), and not at about the third or fourth vertebra down the neck. The incorrect flexion obtained by allowing the horse to flex too far down the neck (or forcing him to do so because he cannot flex at the poll) – even if, as sometimes happens, the front of the face is on the vertical or just in front of it, making this flexion appear correct – ruins the biomechanical effect and the strength of the back. The joints between the vertebrae will be 'opened up' and the whole spine will be in a weaker mode than when the vertebrae are slightly compressed together – rather like a magician's trick wand which keeps collapsing into sections when it is not held correctly. Correct poll flexion makes for a stronger back which is able to sustain collection correctly. Incorrect flexion, which is common nowadays, also prevents the muscles down the underside of the neck and in the chest and shoulders from working to full effect and therefore also hampers foreleg action. So the traditional, classical requirement that a horse flex truly at the poll, with the poll as the highest point of the 'outline', and that he carry the front of his face just slightly in front of the vertical, except in the most advanced movements when it is on the vertical, affects the whole functioning of his spine and muscles and is an essential point of conformation and action to look for. Because so many stallions, which have crested necks, are used in the competitive dressage arena, however, students of conformation must learn to ignore the crest and look just below it at the true line of the neck. Some of these horses are also overweight, which exaggerates the crest. A 'cresty' neck can give the appearance of the highest point of the neck being behind the poll when in fact, the horse *is* flexing correctly at the poll and carrying his head and neck properly. Incorrect work and flexion, however, are very common and it is important to learn to distinguish between right and wrong.

The neck should ideally come out of the shoulders at an angle as close as possible to 45° to the ground. A higher natural neck carriage is acceptable if the horse's poll is very flexible and his throat open, facilitating correct head carriage. If the neck is carried below 45°, however, the horse will tend towards heaviness in hand and to going on the forehand, although this fault can be compensated for if the quarters are strong and correct, as this will facilitate their engagement and a subsequent lifting of the forehand. A common fault relating to head carriage is that very many horses today seem to be purposely trained to go overbent, with the front line of the face actually behind the vertical, making it seem as though the horse is going along looking at the ground, which is wrong, ugly and damaging to a horse's whole movement. It also restricts his vision (because of the way horses' eyes function) and is uncomfortable for him. It is a fault which only seems to have become common over the last decade or so; none of the 'Old Masters' or any of the truly classical teachers today (who are so often respected in theory but ignored in practice) teach this as being correct – indeed they stress that it is *in*correct. I cannot find in any of the classic literature on equitation of this and previous centuries any statement that this posture is correct, although I have found many references to its being wrong.

If a rider has no ambitions to progress beyond the lower levels of competitive dressage, a high-set neck conformation is less important owing to the longer, lower outline required in the earlier stages. However, if the horse is being selected with a view to more advanced work, a naturally, long, low outline will be a decided disadvantage unless the hindquarters compensate, because the horse will be struggling, schooling notwithstanding, to achieve and maintain the higher and more collected carriage needed in advanced competition.

The horse's upper arm or humerus, which runs from the point of the shoulder to the elbow, is very influential in the set and position of the forelegs and their action. It is said that whereas the angle formed by the spine of the shoulder blade with an imaginary line drawn along the length of the horse's side, horizontal to the ground, should be about 45°, that formed by the humerus with that line should be about 60°. If the humerus is set too horizontally, say at a right angle or less to the spine of the shoulder blade, the forelegs may be too far underneath the horse, which will adversely affect his extension and will incline him to be somewhat on the forehand, with consequent stress on the forelegs, however good and straight they are. It will also compromise lightness in hand. If the angle at the point of the shoulder is more obtuse, with a humerus more inclined towards the upright, this will improve matters; however, if a very open angle here is combined with long forearms and short cannons, the gaits will be lower than is normally required for dressage work, resembling more the ground-covering, sweeping stride of the Thoroughbred racehorse or the harness racer. A balance, together with a study of the horse in action, is what is needed.

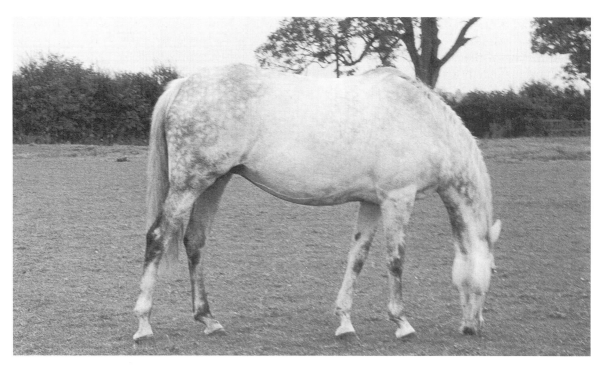

An old gauge of a horse's being well balanced in the forehand was whether or not it could graze comfortably with its forelegs straight

Remember, too, that the forelegs should be straight up and down; when studying the angle at the point of shoulder and the slope of the humerus, if the forelegs slant backward from top to bottom (more common than the reverse slant), the horse will still be 'standing underneath himself' with his forefeet too far back and will show the same difficulties in work as the horse with a too-horizontal humerus, even if the slope of the humerus is in fact good. It is felt generally that horses with fairly open shoulder angles tend to have better overall balance for ridden work.

The horse should look as though he is built naturally slightly 'uphill'. The back should be of medium length or even very slightly on the long side. A very short back usually denotes lack of suppleness both laterally and vertically and a tendency to over-reach, particularly when the horse is young or not fit and muscled up. There must be no tendency to a dipped or sway back nor to an upwardly curved or roach one. From the back of the withers to the loin, the back should run straight and slightly up towards the croup, and the quarters must certainly not be higher than the withers or be too flat, both of which will make it difficult for the horse to lower his quarters and get his hindlegs under him for the propulsion and collection needed. A flat or lumpy wither not only detracts from the appearance and quarters-low conformation but affords insufficient attachment for the muscles of the shoulder and forearm. So, while a noticeably prominent, 'sharp' wither is equally undesirable, if for different reasons (a break in the outline and saddle-fitting problems), it must, if anything, be preferable to a flat one. A 'good' wither between the two is what to look for. An ample wither gives plenty of room for muscle attachment and, if it is a little higher than the croup, will compensate for some deficiencies in the hindquarters. Again, however, overall balance is of prime importance.

The wither should be fairly long from front to back, resulting in a back which looks quite short if the horse is well ribbed up and not slack in the loins (so that you can fit the width of your hand between the last rib and the point of the hip). The withers should flow into the back well behind the top of the shoulder blade otherwise there may be problems of saddle-fit and stability. If the saddle is put on too far forward, the back of the top of the shoulder blade will, with every stride, impact with the front of the saddle, discouraging the horse from using his full freedom of movement in front. In some cases, this can also cause the saddle to be slightly rocked from side to side with each bump from the shoulder blade, which obviously causes the rider, too, to be rocked off centre. The implications of this to a dressage rider, or anyone who wishes to ride correctly and maintain a still, balanced and harmonious seat are obvious. Not only will it adversely affect the rider's seat but it will also create constant, unpleasant, destabilising and unnecessary pressures on the horse's back and affect his balance and muscle use. Putting on the saddle too far forward may also cause the pommel to sit higher than the cantle, shifting the rider back towards the latter and creating an unbalanced seat with the feet probably being forced too far forward because of the set of the stirrup bars, and concentrating her weight too near the horse's loins. The result is difficulty for the rider and considerable discomfort, and disrupted movement, for the horse.

When checking the angle of the shoulder to see whether it is well laid back or well sloped, do not be fooled into letting your eye go from the highest point of the withers to the point of the shoulder. The true line which tells us about the slope of the shoulder is the spine of the shoulder blade which runs down its middle on the side. This can be both seen and felt unless the horse is very fat, and it should be used as the guide. Depending on the height of the individual dorsal spinous processes on the wither vertebrae, the spine may run in front of or behind the highest point of the withers.

When the withers are of good conformation, and the hindquarters are lowered with the hindlegs flexed, the whole of the horse's top line will be gently tensioned, including the muscles of the neck which the horse himself must learn to use to lift his neck up from the base and

forward. This tension will encourage him to do this, and go 'with both ends down and the middle up'.

A smart mover rather than an easy going one is needed for dressage and over-long strides can create problems later when collection is sought. Most horses extend after a fashion more easily and willingly than they collect, although true, correct extension with the horse pushing from behind rather than partially hauling himself along on his forehand is more difficult to achieve. The gaits should be rounded and smooth for competitive dressage, not long and low or high and choppy, and the horse should appear to move on top of the ground, not go down into it. He should, particularly at canter, look as though he would find it easy to sit down, as this makes for an impressive canter with lift in the forehand.

The hindquarters and forehand need to balance each other – strong, thrusting hindquarters are no good if the forehand cannot accept the force – but in any riding horse the hindquarters, the engine, are really more important than the forehand. As I have said, in dressage horses, the position of the hip joint must not be higher than the pivot point of the shoulder blade. The hip joint lies on a straight line just forward from the point of the buttock and one can see it when the horse walks slowly past. Another rule of thumb to help assess hind limb conformation is that a vertical line dropped from the hip joint (not the point of hip) should pass through the tibia or second thigh bone or gaskin and on through the middle of the hoof at the ground. The distance from this line to one dropped from the knee cap at the stifle and a final one dropped from the point of the buttock down the back of the cannon bone should be the same. The ischium or tuber ischi (the end of which bone is called by horse people the point of the buttock) needs to be a reasonable length in order to provide for the muscle attachment and strength needed for power in the canter and for swing in motion.

When choosing a dressage horse, some people go for rather acute angles at stifle and hock, believing that the horse is therefore already half collected and their job half done. In practice, this makes for rather more strain than is experienced by a horse with less acute angles and also tends to produce difficulties when seeking true collection. On the other hand, angles which are too open or obtuse can result in the horse finding it difficult to achieve sufficient flexion for collection and lift.

Longish legs are not a disadvantage to a dressage horse, as they might be to a hunter, a cross-country horse or a hack required to work actively outdoors, for example. The latter need medium-length legs for agility and a centre of balance lower to the ground than a dressage horse who is worked a great deal in a *manège* and needs to produce springy, light gaits (with pasterns of moderate to longish length provided the hoof/pastern axis is straight and the legs and feet are strong). Longish legs, all else being equal, produce lighter gaits and scope.

High School horses

Today there is a significant revival of interest in classical equitation. Although we tend, correctly, to think of the civilisations of ancient Greece and Rome (not forgetting Byzantium) as being the classical era, the principles of classicism were to practise art, literature, conversation, dancing, music, swordsmanship and other cultural and practical pursuits, of which equitation was one, to the highest standards in a *simple, harmonious, restrained style with the aim of lifting the spirits of onlookers and participants*. That definition is most important. When horse people witness *well-performed* classical equitation, many are left awe-struck and with the feeling that they could never do that, but the fact is that most riders and horses can perform the basics of classical equitation, and many the more advanced aspects, with good teaching and a sound, well-conformed horse or pony of almost any type!

Different breeds with tendencies towards different jobs will be described in Chapter 7, including breeds often chosen for High School/classical equitation, but generally there is no set blueprint. The horse does need a natural elegance and a calm temperament – and a commanding presence – if you want to impress audiences, but any well-proportioned and well muscled-up animal can perform well in this work. An open throat with a long poll to enable correct flexion is a big advantage in the more advanced movements, plus a proportionate, well-muscled neck which comes out of the top part of the shoulders at an angle of not less than 45° to the ground. The withers are a moot point as many of the so-called classical breeds have lowish and fairly wide withers, which are not popular today. Well-defined withers of moderate height are a good choice, and the horse must definitely not have his scapular fulcrum or pivot point lower than his hip joint or, indeed, his withers lower than his croup. A moderately 'uphill' build, as for a dressage horse, is a definite plus.

The shoulder needs to be quite long and well sloped and the limbs, particularly the hind limbs, must be strong with good musculature to the upper parts. The hocks must be large, strong and 'flat' from side to side to take the great strain of the ultimate in collection. The body needs to be substantial, with a broad but proportionate chest, a straight, strong, medium-length back, sometimes slightly on the long side, with muscular, wide, short loins leading into very well-muscled hindquarters.

The above conformation is mandatory for the advanced airs, particularly those above the ground, but I have seen everything from mongrel ponies to ex-racehorses execute well what we today call advanced dressage movements (part of a classical repertoire). However, the higher the standard to which you aspire the closer you need to get to the above criteria.

Endurance horses

Endurance riding is today the up-and-coming sport in equestrianism. It is by no means new; endurance tests and races have taken place for thousands of years. But the modern sport has at last received recognition amongst both the veterinary profession, which has obtained a great deal of valuable and hitherto unavailable information on equine exercise physiology as a result of working with endurance horses, and most of the rest of the horse world, which hitherto regarded it as a sport for horses and riders who were incapable of anything else!

The fitness and condition required of endurance horses is very demanding, especially during the longer rides and races, the ultimate currently being 100 miles in twenty-four hours, although lesser distances on two consecutive days are also demanding as the horse must pull out on the second day and complete another longish ride. It is true that there is some misunderstanding amongst riders of the actual biomechanics of riding and of the stresses experienced by the horse, both mental and physical. Because of this, many endurance horses do not appear to be given gymnastic schooling to encourage them to work in trot and canter in a correct, safe outline, with the back raised, the neck stretched up and forward, flexion at the poll (depending on the horse's standard of training), and the quarters lowered and hindlegs able to flex and push the horse along from behind – the normal schooling outline for good development of the 'right' riding muscles.

If they are allowed to go along, as many are, with their heads up, loose reins, backs down and hindquarters and legs trailing out behind them – the exact opposite of a strong and therefore safe way of going – they never develop a supple, curved topline. The muscles along the back become thin, stringy and stiff because they spend insufficient time alternately contracting and being stretched in correct work and use, which permits a healthy blood flow and so promotes a healthy environment within the muscles. Instead, the back muscles tend to stiffen and flatten against the weight of the rider over long periods of time. Rather than taking the form of a strong, convex arc, the spine is more inclined to sag downwards which is a very weak and stressful posture, not at all suitable for carrying weight with minimal stress. This incorrect posture and way of going makes many endurance horses appear to have poor conformation with ewe necks, badly set-on heads and weak backs and hindquarters – one reason why horse people in other sports labelled them as not good enough for anything else.

In fact, successful endurance horses need very strong constitutions, not only to withstand the training necessary to reach the required level of fitness but also, some of them, to work with the disadvantage of being inappropriately ridden. This latter factor is, in my experience, a major contributory cause of back and hindquarter problems and soft tissue injuries in endurance horses.

Those which are ridden correctly at trot and canter, not in an exaggerated way, can swing along perfectly well with a ground-eating stride and withstand the miles and the weight much better and in greater safety from stress injuries. Of course, no one would suggest that it is practicable to maintain an 'outline' constantly for many miles. The horse can 'come off the bit' (to use an expression most people understand) in his periods of walk and should be allowed to stretch along on a long or loose rein. By going correctly, however, endurance horses will become stronger and better fitted to move effectively and do their job successfully for many more years.

Some of the jobs horses do are completely artificial; a leading behaviourist, Dr Marthe Kiley-Worthington, has said that the jobs horses like best are those which most nearly mimic their natural way of life – moving in company at a leisurely pace over open country. Endurance riding often involves horses working in company over open country; however, it certainly does not take place at a leisurely pace or at the horse's free will. Nevertheless, many do enjoy their jobs (although I feel that many of those working over the longer distances do not do so and only carry on because their riders push them or they feel they have no choice). Not all horses are suited to this sport. Endurance horses need very tough constitutions, great natural stamina and acquired physical fitness. Although it is said that any sound, fit horse or pony should be able to complete rides successfully at the lower to medium distances, at the top end of the sport, temperament, way of going, constitution and usually a medium size (in the 15 hands range) are essential.

The horse needs a ground-covering stride at all gaits, the trot being regarded as of the utmost importance which is rather strange because it is the gait least used by horses in the wild, who migrate at a walk or canter; perhaps more consideration could be given to this topic. The action must be straight and neat so that the horse is not in danger of hitting himself nor of using up too much energy with unnecessary flamboyance. High natural cruising speeds are desirable in each gait and the gaits must

A successful endurance horse whose natural stance is to toe out, like this. He competes frequently, is never sick, sorry or lame and copes with his natural imperfection without incident

obviously be comfortable to sit to. A tough constitution and tip-top, all-round health are most important. Heart, lungs, feet and legs come to mind first, but every bodily system must work at peak efficiency. Conformation should comply with the classical ideal described earlier but, once again, individual harmony and symmetry are what to look for first. Good muscling, straight limbs, powerful quarters, deep girth, hard hooves and plenty of room for the windpipe in the jowl area are the other important points to check. Long backs are out for endurance horses. Medium to shortish backs denote the strength to carry a rider for many miles at a sometimes tough, fast pace. This make and shape will usually result in the horse being a lean, wiry type and close-coupled, not slack in the loins, which causes unnecessary weakness and stress.

Size does vary but generally, the most successful endurance horses are smallish horses and ponies. A compact animal, or one roughly 14.3–15.3 hands will fit the bill.

Event horses

The event horse used to be known as a jack of all trades because of the need to be good at dressage, cross-country, sometimes steeplechasing, and showjumping. In fact, it needs a special kind of animal to excel in the three major Olympic disciplines of dressage, cross-country and showjumping. But many top eventers could just as easily have had successful careers as steeplechasers or point-to-pointers and there is virtually no difference in the required conformation for both sports.

An ideal height seems to be between 16 and 17 hands. At the higher levels today, smaller horses will not usually have the speed and scope, and larger ones may not be sufficiently agile to cope with the ups and downs and twists and turns of the cross-country courses. Thoroughbred or seven-eighths TB horses are best, with strength, scope, speed and power. The horse needs to be an all-round athlete and his temperament must be such that he can perform an accurate, impressive dressage test on the first day (for events over more than one day) whilst being fully tuned up, fit and raring to go for the steeple-chase, if appropriate, and the cross-country on the next day. Then, after the exertions of those two phases, he must be fit and sound enough, not to mention calm, energetic and controllable enough, to perform a creditable showjumping round on the third day. The order of phases changes according to the level and type of competition, but basically the requirements of temperament are just as important as the horse's physical conformation. In short, the horse needs a willing, calm, enthusiastic and not phlegmatic nature.

An obvious, desirable starting point is a conformation that is as correct as possible. The horse also needs stamina and the ability to combine jumping ability with speed so as to complete the cross-country course in as near the optimum time as possible. Substance is essential to withstand the rigours of the training and of competing itself.

The action must be straight and economical, as anything else uses up vital energy and inclines the horse to interfering and difficulty in getting himself and his rider out of sticky spots. Top riders and trainers usually go for a Thoroughbred-type gait with fairly long and low, sweeping strides, rather than a high, rounded action, as the former carries speed with it. However, some height in the action and knee and hock movement is needed so that the horse can cope with the various water hazards and also lift his feet out of possibly deep or tricky going. Good legs and feet are crucial, plus agility and nimbleness to avoid falls and to jump economically but at speed.

A strong, sound constitution and an excellent cardiac-respiratory system are essential but not easy to assess at purchase; some knowledge of the horse and his history are a definite advantage when buying an eventer!

Showjumpers

As I have said, showjumpers come in all sorts of shapes and sizes and are often impossible to pick out just by looking. One thing which is essential and which has nothing to do with conformation is temperament; all the talent in the world is useless if the horse has an uncontrollable temperament. Showjumpers *must* be amenable, keen to listen to the rider but, ideally, also quick-thinking enough to get the partnership out of trouble. Many an event horse, for instance, has come unstuck in the showjumping phase of that sport because he either 'hots up', argues with his rider or regards the artificial-looking obstacles with disdain. Showjumpers must hate touching fences! They need a calm, intelligent temperament which does not 'hot up' against the clock.

A workmanlike rather than a showy action is preferred, with athletic use of the limbs and a natural inclination to fold the front legs right up and to lift the knees at the same time. Otherwise the horse will have to lift his body significantly higher than necessary to clear his fences, which is a waste of energy and may demand an ability he does not have. Nowadays, showjumpers are often sought which actually stretch their legs out over big spreads. The hocks must be noticeably flexed to help get the back end over without dragging a toe and collecting faults. Any crowd-pleasing antics such as kicking out as the horse comes down the arc or bucking on landing are not, actually, a point in the horse's favour. A kick-out has been known to lose valuable purses for the riders of more than one such horse and these sorts of actions often indicate back pain in the horse or pain in the forefeet. Jumping low fences on an occasional basis can be regarded as a natural occupation for the horse family in its natural surroundings and jumping ability is felt by many to be a remnant of the time when the horse's ancestors were forest-dwelling animals, but it must be admitted that negotiating very high fences is completely unnatural and undoubtedly creates many stresses and resultant injuries on the horse's body.

Training plays a great part in performance and bringing out a horse's natural ability but the horse selected for this sport must show a natural bascule (arcing action) over fences if any success is to be achieved at even the mid-range of this sport. A horse endowed with this movement as a natural attribute will help to provide those vital extra inches when the chips are down.

As in all horses, the walk is crucial, even though horses do not normally jump in competition out of walk! (I once spent an entertaining half-hour watching an Olympic showjumper school his horses over 4 ft fences out of walk. 'If they can't do this,' he explained, 'they're no good for this job.') The showjumper must have a smooth, active walk with particularly strong hindquarters (as the propulsive force), and with the hind hooves over-tracking the fore.

The question of jumper's bumps is worth considering, even though many of the best showjumpers in the world do not show this conformation. A jumper's bump is simply a prominent croup, and some people think this must mean that there is extra bone formation for the attachment of more muscle to assist in the upward thrust on take-off at an obstacle. The top line of a horse is usually required to consist of pleasing curves running into each other and forming a smooth, undulating shape. A prominent croup which still shows an attractive top line is termed a jumper's bump. The muscle masses on top of the hindquarters are attached to the pelvis, the rear part of the spine and the thighs. The loin or lumbar region also provides strength and space for the attachment of large, powerful muscles. Short but wide loins and longish, deep hindquarters should indicate good musculature in a normally conditioned horse, or

good potential in a horse in poorer condition. The tail should be set on at the level of the horse's back. In post-mortems, so-called jumper's bumps are often found to be nothing more than a slight excess of bone formation on the top parts of the pelvis; but extra bone formation *can* mean extra space for muscle attachment!

What is *not* required is a similar conformation called a 'goose rump', which is sometimes confused with a jumper's bump. In a goose rump, a horse usually has a short, poorly muscled and weak-looking hindquarter with the hind part (behind the croup) sloping downwards fairly steeply to a tail set lower than the back. This is not the same thing at all as a jumper's bump, despite the prominent croup, and does not bode well for the horse's ability as a jumper because he is unlikely to have the strength of hindquarter to jump well.

The forehand, too, must move freely and the shoulders must be free and mobile to help provide the agility needed and to enable the horse to stretch up and out from the shoulder and humerus, not just from the elbow, to lift his forehand and forelegs over poles which are only too ready to fall.

When trying out a potential purchase over a small fence, note whether or not he looks where he is going and whether he approaches his obstacle with purpose and intent, yet is able to complete his test easily and not treat it as though it were a big or worrying job. The horse's hindquarters should appear to thrust him effortlessly upward, with the shoulders lifting easily and all the legs flexing neatly. The head and neck must be used naturally to balance the body during the bascule, and the whole action should seem to be strong and smooth. Look particularly for any tendency to refuse, run out or look too hard at the fence (to which the vendor should have accustomed the horse), and watch for twisting over the fence, kicking out, bucking and ears laid back with a stressed expression on landing. All these things can indicate physical pain, usually in the back or feet, although they can also indicate that the horse has been over-jumped and over-faced. With these faults, you are already at a disadvantage.

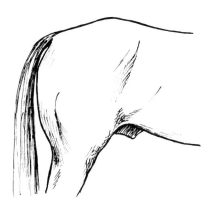

A jumper's bump which often, at first glance, gives the impression of poor hindquarter musculature. Jumpers' bumps usually indicate slightly excess bone formation which allows extra attachment space for muscles in the hindquarters which, of course, power the horse over his jumps

Carriage-driving horses

Those not familiar with driving horses often imagine that carriage driving, even the active 'eventing' version of the sport, is fairly sedate, with no particular stress on the horses. There is also an attitude amongst some that driving horses must be in harness because they are not good enough to ride. Nothing could be further from the truth. Competitive carriage driving is a tough sport needing a tough horse – or five of them if you want to go in for the ultimate in this sport, four-in-hand competition driving (the fifth horse being essential as a reserve). The more horseflesh you have the more likelihood there is of something going wrong with some of it. The sport is therefore an expensive one in which to participate at any level, but particularly in World Championships.

Carriage horses need to be strong and compact, with plenty of substance and particularly good legs (not too fine) and feet. The favoured height is between 15 and 16 hands, for speed with agility. The shoulder needs to be slightly more upright than in a riding horse (although many are ridden as it is more practicable, on a daily basis, to give the horses some fitness work under saddle rather than having to harness up and put to every time they need to be exercised or worked). The reason for the more upright shoulder is to make it more comfortable for the horse to lean into his collar and really push his weight against it. Because the horses obviously push their vehicles along rather than truly pulling them, the hindquarters and hindlegs of a driving horse are just as vital as those of a riding horse because they are the horse's engine. Weak hindlegs often develop curbs (injury to and subsequent thickening of the plantar ligament) just below the point of the hock on the back of the leg as a result of the constant stress of the horse pushing his own weight and that of his vehicle (and its load). Heavy haulage horses were, and still can be, particularly prone to this injury but competition carriage horses are less commonly affected.

The quarters must be strong and naturally well muscled (work-induced development notwithstanding); they should not be too short because good length is needed for ample muscle mass and attachment. The thighs and second thighs must also be well muscled and the horse must certainly not be 'cut up behind' so that the muscles between the thighs under the tail do not meet, unless he is in very poor condition and underweight. The quarters must have an even hip height and a strong, squarish appearance from behind with plenty of width throughout (from top to bottom when viewed from behind).

A shortish back is desirable, but not so short that the horse tends to over-reach and injure his fore heels with his hind toes. He needs a good front with a fairly long shoulder and a slightly, or even markedly, prominent croup and slightly sloping quarter to enable him to get his hindlegs underneath him and push. Any tendency towards a weak goose rump, however, should be avoided. A middle road may be safest: look for quarters which are not flat (for competition driving where real hard, physical work is done) and which have good muscling combined with size and strength.

Strange though it may seem, the horse's pushing power will be enhanced if he has a well set-on head and neck. This is so that he can be trained and encouraged to go in the traditional, correct, strong and therefore safe way with his head and neck stretched up and forward and his poll and lower jaw flexed. Just because a horse goes in harness and is not required to perform under saddle, it does not mean that one can get away with hammer heads, sharp throat angles, ewe necks and 'star gazing' – certainly at the higher levels of the sport. A correct way of going will do nothing but help a carriage horse – another reason why it is a good idea to school him correctly under saddle. His top line should be just as smooth and flowing, within his shape, as that of a riding horse and he should present a curved outline, big, rounded and well muscled-up even when very fit for the top levels of competition. Good riding and driving technique will enhance this appearance and the job will be made much more difficult if the attitude is adopted that good, normal, balanced make and shape are unnecessary for a harness horse.

A driving horse must have a free, swinging, ground-covering walk, with the ability to lengthen and shorten stride naturally at the request of his driver. Long, free strides are also needed in trot and slight but noticeable knee action is required (although a little less than in the days when carriage horses were genuinely used for transport and had to cope with deep mud). A certain showiness and cadence is a definite advantage in the dressage, with elegance and straightness, not flamboyance. The knee action will make for an attractive appearance in this phase of competition as well as helping the horse cope with uneven and difficult ground conditions in the endurance phase.

These horses do not work in canter except for short stints now and then to make up time.

Private driving

Horses used for this extremely elegant sport do not need the same tough constitution as competitive carriage-driving horses, but they should be elegant, even beautiful, with a sound, balanced conformation, an attractive colour or eye-catching markings. Straight action is still needed, as otherwise the horse will be prone to interfering and injuring himself as he manoeuvres his vehicle. Today, many private driving clubs hold rallies and drives which involve trotting for several miles on hard roads and therefore very good legs and well-conformed feet are needed to cope with the concussion. It seems that many such horses are allowed, even encouraged, to trot too fast which is always potentially injurious but especially on a hard surface.

A Hackney mare of yesteryear (note the docked tail), showing the high head carriage, lean rather long body, long powerful hindquarters and long, refined legs of the breed. The feet are left longer than most of us would wish to encourage the mare to lift her feet in the characteristic high Hackney action

The horse should have a moderately long neck with good musculature, a fairly sloping and long shoulder and strong limbs, well muscled and not too fine, and very good feet. A broad chest is needed in front of a wide, deep girth, a short, straight back and muscular loins and hindquarters.

Specific breeds used in this type of carriage work have their own natural action. Spanish Andalusians, for instance, are known for dishing and are actually bred to do it as the horsemen of their natural homeland regard it as showy and attractive. English Hackneys have an instantly recognisable high, reaching, springy and cadenced action which marks them out immediately from any other breed, but which was selectively bred for appearance (and enhanced by training) and would distinctly hamper its owner in competition carriage driving. However, Hackney horses and ponies which are not trained to enhance their natural action, resulting in their familiar, exaggerated show-ring action, make fine harness horses and are up to a lot of work.

There are various branches of show driving, with classes for types, for breeds, and for horses doing or originally bred for particular jobs such as vanners and costermongers' horses and ponies. The only way to become familiar with them all is to visit shows and events where they are being exhibited. For any discipline, though, the basic criteria of a balanced overall conformation and straight action of the type desired remain essential.

Heavy horses

Heavy haulage work, farm work and work in industry are not quaint aspects of horses' work: many countries of the world still use horses for this kind of work, including many in the Western world. Brewery horses are still common, and not only in the form of show teams. Heavy horses are still used in work situations in Europe (very much so in eastern Europe, Russia and neighbouring countries) and are being re-introduced in the U.K. as the ideal vehicle for such jobs as council work and haulage in forests (where in most cases they have never been ousted by machinery), national parks and a few farms. In North America, heavy horses are not at all uncommon in work and show situations, and lighter heavies, cobs and the heavier types of ponies are used for tourist transport, estate work and farm work in many countries. The elegant delivery horses of London, not to mention the courier horses of Buckingham Palace, are a much-admired part of the city's life.

As far as the true 'heavies' are concerned, their very meatiness has led to a situation where some breeds' main purpose is the provision of horsemeat for the dining table in many continental European countries. Their massive musculature, heavy bone structure, shorter legs (except for many present-day Shires, Clydesdales and Percherons) with a wide, stable ground-base and a huge hoof at each corner, make these horses slow, immensely strong, very stable and well balanced. There are some heavy horse breeds (see Chapter 7) which are slow and almost never work out of a walk but others are more lively and energetic and pull heavy loads at a relatively smart trot. All heavy breeds, however, tend to have large heads, usually described as 'noble', and usually with a convex (Roman) nose. This by no means always denotes a dull, stupid temperament however; many heavy breeds have, over the years, had a dash of hot blood added for quality, usually Arabian, notably the Percheron.

The neck should be short, thick and muscular, the shoulder fairly upright and powerful, the limbs short for effective draught and overall balance, with very short cannons, and solid with muscular forearms and, particularly, thighs and gaskins. The joints need to be large, 'flat' and not at all puffy. The body should be very compact with a broad, powerful chest, wide and deep girth, short back with a well ribbed-up mid section, short, wide, strong loins and very muscular croup and rump.

The feet of heavy breeds are usually large but can be rather flat. For show-ring appearance, feet have been bred into many heavy horses which are too small for the body, and this is a definite defect. The show ring has a lot to answer for, in all species.

Harness racers

Harness pacers and trotters are some of the toughest and grittiest horses you can find. They need great speed and stamina (a harness racer can reach speeds equal to a galloping Thoroughbred) and a long and well-muscled neck. The use of the neck, though, is greatly hampered by the use of a tight bearing rein which also stiffens the back and discourages the horse from putting his head down and breaking into canter, which would disqualify him. The shoulder is long, powerful and sloping and the legs long and well-muscled, with long upper legs, short cannons and sloping pasterns to help absorb the considerable force on the legs. The chest needs to be broad with a deep, wide girth, a long, straight back and muscular hindquarters. Many harness racers, however, tend towards long cannons and short backs, which are a weakness and, in trotters, a source of potential injury from over-reaching. Some are croup high and some trotters carry their hindfeet outside their forefeet to avoid over-reaching and injuring themselves.

Flat racers

A well-conformed, middle- to long-distance flat-racing Thoroughbred is regarded by many horse people as the epitome of the perfect riding horse and some will not ride anything else – and there are plenty to be had, as about 5000 a year leave racing in the U.K. alone although, of course, a lot of these have physical and mental problems due to the stress of their racing lives.

Sprinters, which include Thoroughbreds who race under a mile as well as the fastest horses in the world, American Quarter Horses (which are said to hold their breath for as long as they are flying over their quarter-mile distances!), need very compact bodies with moderately long legs and sloping pasterns, with feet large enough to take the force of the extreme power generated. They should be very well muscled-up due to the extreme power they need to get off to a standing start, reach their top speed in about four seconds and to work those low-oxidative fast-twitch muscles anaerobically. Strong hindquarters, thighs and gaskins are especially important for

the great thrust needed, plus well-muscled, laid-back shoulders and free elbows for reach in front. The neck should be long and well muscled for balance, the chest well muscled and the girth deep, and the horse should have a moderately long back, short, wide and muscular loins and big, muscular hindquarters.

An interesting trend developed in the 1970s in American Thoroughbred sprinters (which are bred exclusively for great speed) of long hindlegs and croup-high quarters with a characteristic rump-swinging gait brought about by having to carry their hindfeet outside their forefeet, sometimes even in walk, to avoid injuring themselves. A further development seems to be rather long backs to compensate for this. These physical characteristics are particularly interesting because they themselves are not selected for but are the result of features necessary for extreme speed, which *is* selected for.

Middle- to long-distance flat racers, normally Thoroughbreds but also increasingly Arabians, need a much leaner build, more like a greyhound, for the longer distances over which they race. The Thoroughbreds usually have tremendous fronts, often with excellent, long withers, long, lean but well-developed necks for balance and very deep girths and good chests for lung and heart room, and appear to have more oval-shaped ribcages just behind the shoulder but 'well-sprung' bodies behind the rider. They should have moderately long backs, the usual wide, short and muscular loins and big hindquarters well covered with lean muscle.

A major fault with most flat racers, it seems, is, flat, shelly feet in Thoroughbreds and feet which are sometimes too small for the body in Quarter Horses.

Arabian flat racers are a still-evolving type in modern terms; as they race over longer distances, they also need the greyhound-type build and it will be interesting to watch the development of their type in the future.

Steeplechasers and point-to-pointers are very like long-distance flat-racing Thoroughbreds in conformation but usually have a more substantial build for their very tough sport, epitomising sleek, strong lines. They usually have great fronts, longish backs and longish, very hard and tough legs with big, well-muscled (but not chunky) hindquarters for jumping power. The second thigh bones from stifle to hock in particular should be long for great leverage and the forelegs need to be perfect in order to withstand the concussion of landing from big fences at speed. Over-long pasterns and weak tendons soon put paid to a jumper's career.

Hurdlers are often failed flat racers (Thoroughbreds) but the best are specialists in their field and very high-quality horses. Hurdle races consist of low, knock-down brush hurdles which horses must negotiate at speed – faster than steeplechasers – and good hurdlers are, indeed, fast horses with the type of conformation seen in middle- to long-distance flat-racing Thoroughbreds with good jumping hindlegs and hindquarters.

Barrel racers, cutting horses and reining horses

The reason these three types of horse are mentioned together is because the same basic conformation applies to them all. The disciplines are mainly American but are also popular in Australia and some other countries where horses are commonly used to work stock. The competitions stem from the actual work of ranch horses, some of which are more suited to the different jobs than others, as in any sphere. Many working stock horses also compete but the required temperamental and conformational qualities are the same whatever the situation.

Barrel racers are required to race against time, twisting and turning around three spaced barrels placed in a triangular or clover-leaf pattern. The idea is to demonstrate the horse's agility and speed in a competitive setting.

Cutting horses work with cattle and are required to 'cut out' or separate selected animals from the herd, with no signal of any kind from the rider (telepathic communication!). Many horses which are good at stock work have an inborn 'cow sense', known as having 'a lot of cow', and must think out and plan their own strategies in work and competition. Accuracy and speed are essential in the competition. The

horse must also have a temperament which enables it to move slowly and unobtrusively amongst the herd without disturbing it and then quickly and firmly cut out a selected animal to a separate area for some kind of treatment. His job is not then finished, though, as the horse, again without any cue or help from the rider (who must be very well balanced and himself have 'a lot of horse' in order to stay with his mount), must prevent the animal from returning to the herd by blocking its lightning darts, twists and turns with matching rapid movements of his own.

Reining horses' work is again based on ranch work and is devised to show the horse's willingness, agility and speed and, obviously, his skill at neck reining. This calls for a very well-schooled, balanced horse, contrary to popular opinion amongst horse enthusiasts who have never experienced it. The competitions are run over complicated patterns and test the horse's flexibility, knowledge, intelligence and willingness to the ultimate. He is judged on time and effectiveness in changing legs (leads), turning, stopping and reining back (backing up), also on balance, obedience to the rider and the maintenance of calmness at all times.

For all three of these types of horse, the conformation of a sprint racer is ideal with the exception of the barrel racer. A short to medium-length back is needed, very tough, strong legs and feet with good muscling in the upper limbs and the ability to get the hindlegs and hindquarters well under the body. The horse must be completely light in hand and able to go in perfect balance independently of the rider; this work is no place for heavy bit contact – hardly appropriate in a western curb, anyway. Because of this, excellent conformation and function of head and neck are essential. The legs and feet must be near perfect because of the considerable stress placed on them.

Polo ponies

Equines used for polo are always called ponies no matter what their height. An animal of about 14.3–15.3 hands is needed for handiness, plus the substance needed for the rough and tumble of this game. Polo is probably the oldest horse sport in the world apart from racing; there are official records of games and results from 500 BC, and it was probably well established much earlier than that. The heads of dead enemies were often used in the past, but today balls suffice.

The game is extremely fast and many purists, probably justifiably, bemoan the passing of the days when polo ponies were well schooled, and very light in hand, when they played in pelhams or double bridles and when martingales, and certainly standing martingales, were not only hardly ever seen but recognised as the mark of an incompetent rider. Today, things are very different. There is a lot of money in the game and it is very much faster and tougher than it was a couple of generations and more ago. Today's polo ponies are routinely fitted out in gags, drop nosebands, cavesson nosebands to take a standing martingale, breastplates and often running reins, all to help the rider get instantaneous control and response without question or hesitation from his pony.

The game is played on a grass field or ground (although in hot, dry countries hardly a blade of grass is seen), measuring 4 hectares (10 acres), and up to 275 m (300 yards) in length by 183 m (200 yards) in width, although if boards are used to define the playing area and help keep the ball in play the width may be reduced to 146 m (160 yards). There are two sets of goal posts 7 m (8 yards) apart and the goals must be no more than 228 m (250 yards) apart. The game is played by teams of four mounted players (it is also played on elephants, camels and bicycles) in six periods or chukkas of 7$\frac{1}{2}$ minutes. The players have mallets (sticks) with which to hit a ball only 8 cm (3$\frac{1}{4}$ in) in diameter and 156 g (5$\frac{1}{2}$ oz) in weight up and down the ground with the aim of getting it between the opposition's goalposts as often as possible (there is no goalkeeper).

Because of the inherent danger of the game to riders and ponies from the sticks, balls, collisions, falls, treads and so on, the ponies must be very brave, completely obedient and fast to gallop after the ball. They must have plenty of

intelligence and ball sense, be determined and tough enough to 'ride off' or shoulder away an opponent's pony – and do all this without 'hotting up'. It is a tall order indeed and it is no wonder that the best ponies fetch the same sorts of prices as high-class racehorses.

The qualities of toughness, agility, handiness for the constant starts, stops and turns, acceleration, great sprinting speed and power are all essential in a polo pony. One may be forgiven for thinking that typical sprinting make and shape are required but, surprisingly, this is not the case and the breeding of polo ponies (which are a type, not a breed) has been refined down to a fine art, especially in Argentina where polo is a way of life among horse people.

A rather short back (not generally associated with great comfort for the rider – which does not matter in this sport) is preferred as this facilitates agility on the field. Because polo is definitely a contact sport, a moderately substantial build is needed, but without any hint of coarseness. The pony also needs a well-balanced body for the constant twists, turns, stops and starts of the game, a deep chest – certainly not narrow – for lung and heart room, and a head and neck set on well, not too low in front. Points to be avoided are a hammer-headed or ewe-necked head carriage which will cause the horse to be above the bit or, conversely, a swan neck or low neck conformation, particularly with a head that is at all large, as this will produce a natural inclination to go behind the bit. Both of these faults make control and manoeuvrability difficult.

Long, sloping shoulders and moderately high withers are needed to help keep the saddle in place because the rider spends a good deal of time leaning out over the side of it. A well-defined girth groove behind the elbows is a definite asset for the same reason, although ponies nearly always wear breastplates or breastgirths and sometimes, although not usually in high goal polo, cruppers as well.

Moderately long legs with well-muscled upper parts are needed for speed with agility, and slightly shorter, more upright pasterns than are normally required in riding horses, as they are less prone to tendon strain. A well-sprung, well ribbed-up barrel is essential, with well-muscled quarters, tough feet and excellent natural balance. Polo ponies, then, have the qualities of a sprinter yet, to look at, are very different. They are now a type of their own, at least in high-goal polo where the pace is fastest and toughest. Once the game is in progress, the welfare of the ponies comes second to scoring goals and the ponies have to be able to take being knocked and pulled about by their peers and their riders, being hit by ball and mallet and brushing it all off with equanimity. This is one category of sport horse where the ability to neck-rein is a must.

Show horses

The world of showing, like many equestrian disciplines, is a world of its own – wheels within wheels – and there are many different breeds and types of horse and pony, most of which are instantly identifiable by horse enthusiasts, even if they are not of the type with which they are involved. Different countries have their own types of show horse and it is neither possible nor necessary to describe the conformation of them all here, just the main ones. Breeds, as opposed to types, are described in Chapter 7 – and a horse can be both. For instance many a good Ladies' Hunter or Hack is full Thoroughbred or Anglo-Arab and many a Middleweight Hunter is Irish Draught or largely so.

Showing in general can form an invaluable part of the education of almost any horse and it is well worth sorting out every suitable class for a young or green horse, even if the show ring is not his intended destiny.

Cobs are probably the most English/Irish type of equines in the world. They are difficult to define yet impossible to mistake and have a type and character all their own. A true ride and drive animal, the show cob is always regarded as a riding animal. If you had to choose one word to describe his physical appearance you would probably choose 'stocky'. Neither refined nor coarse, they are of medium weight and ooze character and quality, and whilst they are usually placid and reliable they have a great sense of

humour. They are ideal for all-purpose riding – for the young, the old, the not-so-athletic, the not-so-confident, yet also for those who want an active yet safe time on board. They are suitable for general riding, pleasure riding or hacking, harness work and also hunting.

The show-ring height limit is 15.1 hands. The head should be workmanlike and attractive and show an intelligent, perceptive quality, with large, generous eyes. The mane and forelock are always hogged (roached) for the show ring and the tail pulled and banged. The neck should be short and strong, shapely and set on the top part of the chest/shoulders. The withers are of moderate definition but the shoulders are long, sloping and powerful. The back is usually short, the loins wide, short and strong, the body deep and close-coupled to the hindquarters, which are rounded and muscular with the tail not high set. The chest and girth area needs to be wide and deep (yet comfortable to sit on) and the legs sturdy (neither fine nor heavy – feather is trimmed off for show), with very short cannons and long, muscular forearms, gaskins and thighs. The pasterns of many cobs tend to be short so look for slightly longer ones, making a moderate length above rounded, hard feet of proportionate size.

The problem with cobs is that they cannot be bred with any certainty. Even cobs as breeds, such as the Welsh Cob, do not always produce cobs when mated outside their breed. It is often found that Welsh Cob or Irish Draught blood somewhere in the ancestry will produce a show-type cob but generally you have to snap them up when they occur as their breeding is one of Nature's mysteries.

The Show Pony is today such a well-established type that it is instantly recognisable, like most specific category horses and ponies. It is a quality riding pony which used to be just like a miniature Thoroughbred and just as hot; nowadays, the temperament has improved and so has the fineness – the animals are more robust yet still with 'class'. They range from 12.2–14.2 hands, the more Thoroughbred types being found in the larger heights. Their conformation is that of a quality riding horse but the head and face, and the character, must be definitely pony and not horse.

Riding or Pleasure Horses in any country normally have their specific classes and fit into identifiable types. Western Pleasure Horses are, as the name implies, good riding horses which will go under western tack and in the outline or frame of their class stipulations. British and Irish Riding Horses are quality animals which may be too big or not have the class for Hack classes yet not be of Show Hunter type, either. Horses which are midway between the two classes abound and the best are very desirable animals. They usually have much Thoroughbred blood and their conformation fits into the general blueprint given earlier.

The Show Hack of various categories (Ladies', Small, Large) is a peculiarly British and Irish phenomenon and although there is currently a paucity of really refined and properly schooled

A useful, workmanlike type of riding horse with an honest face, perhaps a slightly short neck, but an otherwise well-balanced conformation with good, straight legs and feet

animals, this is possibly a temporary decline. The hack, and particularly the Ladies' Hack, must be the epitome of quality, of near perfect Thoroughbred or Anglo-Arab type and conformation, have impeccable manners and be beautifully schooled, ideally to go easily when ridden with one hand so that a gentleman may raise his hat (in the days when they were not locked on) and a lady wave to her friends when out riding. The conformation must be more or less Thoroughbred in type, with a very refined head and natural presence. Substance and notable strength are not needed but fluid, light and airy gaits are. The whole picture should be one of manners, elegance and top quality.

Show Hunters are ridden by the judge but are never jumped in Britain or Ireland, although the reverse is the case in the U.S.A. Although a hunter is technically any horse on which one can ride to hounds, the Show Hunter is a very specific type which, like the other show types, can only really be recognised by looking at and getting a feel for the entrants at good shows, particularly those in the ribbons.

The Show Hunter, even in the Lightweight class (there are also Ladies', Mediumweight and Heavyweight classes), needs substance with excellent riding conformation and must look as though it has the stamina for a long day with hounds, which will be typified by plenty of lung and heart room (a deep girth and reasonably broad chest and ribcage). The body needs to be strong with only a moderately long back and with powerful hindquarters. The legs must not in any way be spindly but strong with very short cannons and well-muscled forearms, gaskins and thighs. The feet, too, must be of a good size for the horse with a correct hoof–pastern axis and moderately long pasterns. The horse must look naturally well balanced and have straight, powerful action. A ground-covering action at the gallop must be displayed in the show ring, plus the willingness to pull up easily.

The Working Hunter category started life as the poor relation of the Show Hunter but is now a respected type of its own. Workmanlike riding horse conformation is needed, like the Show Hunter, but perhaps without quite the same quality. Jumping ability in free-going but calm hunting style is definitely needed with strong, ground-covering action.

There are also *Working Hunter Pony* and *Riding Pony of Hunter Type* classes of animals for young riders and basically the same qualities are needed as for the adult Working Hunters and Show Hunters, but with definite pony character, typified normally in the head and way of going.

Young competition horses must conform to the make and shape of horses competing in their intended discipline. It should always be borne in mind, though, that many animals of good, even superb, conformation (and action, which is discussed in Chapter 6) can perform well in several disciplines. Most top event horses would make excellent steeplechasers and point-to-pointers and vice versa and not a few event horses have retired from eventing to take up showjumping. Many racehorses, both flat horses and jumpers, go on to have other careers if they are sound enough and can be psychologically re-educated, and almost any sound horse or pony can take up any kind of hunting – you do not have to jump fences to hunt as shown by the numbers of little children and the elderly who go out on their ponies and cobs and are adept at finding gaps, gates and short cuts.

Faults in drawing of horse with poor conformation: rather heavy head making for poor balance and a horse on the forehand; sharp angle at throat causing difficulty in flexing; thick, heavy neck which may be inflexible; loaded shoulder making for rolling movement; fore tendons tied in below the knee which indicates weakness; rather short front pasterns which may produce a rough ride; small, very shallow feet which will probably cause constant shoeing and maybe lameness problems; a roach back which is strong but uncomfortable to sit on and may push the saddle forward into the backs of the shoulders and behind the elbows, particularly as there is no girth groove and the withers are fairly low; weak gaskins and long hind cannons. Maybe his temperament will make him an ideal companion or pet because he'll never be any good for real work

CHAPTER

6

CONFORMATION IN ACTION

Enough has probably been said already in this book for readers to appreciate how very important a horse's action is. His conformation is also important but because horses in our society are bred to be more or less athletic animals, some of them very athletic indeed, it is the way that their conformation translates into movement that finally decides whether or not they are suitable for a particular purpose. It can be very disappointing to see a photograph of a potential purchase, to take the time, trouble and expense of going to see him, to admire him stood up in the yard and then to be brought down to earth with a bump because his action does not fulfil the promise of his conformation. Perhaps we should all be asking for videos as a matter of course, not just photographs, when looking for a potential equine athlete.

Some general thoughts on movement

The horse is a 'rear-wheel-drive' animal: he pushes himself along from the back with his hindlegs and hindquarters, although if he is not correctly ridden or is suffering discomfort or pain from an injury or stiffness, badly fitting tack or harness, poor riding or driving or being forced to move in a way he finds uncomfortable or distressing, he may well learn to at least partially haul himself along from the front end. This will result in incorrect muscle development, usually along the underside of the neck and

behind the shoulder blades. Other physical evasions may occur, such as twisting and not going straight.

The horse has four natural gaits: walk, trot, canter and gallop. The gaits most used by the horse at liberty are walk and canter. These are the favoured gaits when horses are on the move from one grazing ground to another or trekking to watering sources. Trot is used mainly to put on a little speed over very short distances such as moving away from a rejecting herd mate or catching up with a friend, also during play. Gallop and canter are used in play, and gallop is, of course, the horse's main line of defence for escaping from danger.

Bearing that in mind, and remembering that horses have natural cruising speeds in any gait and will automatically change gait when they reach a speed at which a different gait would be more economical in oxygen and energy use, it seems inappropriate that trot is used a great deal as a ground-covering gait by endurance riders and for schooling by dressage riders and others.

It would seem well worth while for endurance riders perhaps to concentrate more on developing the natural migration gait – canter – with the horse in a gently rounded outline, head inclined down, hindquarters and hindlegs tending to come underneath and the back slightly arched up, allowing him to swing along relatively effortlessly in his natural canter cruising speed. I do not mean, of course, that he should never trot or that he should be asked to go along actually 'on the bit' or 'in an outline', for want of better expressions, for mile after mile, but he should at least be asked to move in a safer, stronger and more upwardly convex shape and without the use of martingales or other aids. Certainly he should not be allowed to spank along completely disengaged in trot and canter with his hindlegs strung out behind, his back down and his head and neck up. Of course endurance riders want to cover the ground and may understandably feel that letting the horse go in his natural way, without undue interference, is the best way to do it. However, his natural way is *not* carrying a sixth or more of his own weight at a fast or fairly fast pace in each gait and it is also not natural for him to use trot for longish distances. Therefore, the rider can help the horse a great deal by encouraging him to move in a way which will help to protect him from the unnatural elements of weight and sustained speed.

Schooling at home a few times a week, even twenty minutes several days a week, in a school or out hacking (where a lot of good work can be done without nagging or drilling the horse) in correct, gymnastic ways of going, partly using poles and other groundwork, and without outline-fixing devices such as draw-reins and tight side-reins, will bring about a considerable improvement in the horse's movement, strength, speed and stamina.

When schooling horses in basic flatwork – which is essential for every discipline – I feel a lot more work should be done in that very important gait, the walk, than normally seems to be the case. In fact, many excellent trainers and teachers do not let their equine or human students work in a faster gait until they have mastered various principles and movements and can reliably get a horse working well, in walk, according to the horse's level of training.

As far as schooling is concerned, more work in walk will greatly help improve the trot and canter work. There is no point in trying to canter before the horse can trot, or trot before he can walk! It would also be a good idea if dressage tests stipulated less time in trot, more in demonstrating training and movements in a really

good walk and more in canter. Also, more time should be stipulated in the horse's natural 'gear' within a gait, making tests less stressful by reducing (if not eliminating) the demand for types of gait which are slower or faster than the horse would naturally choose. Much more emphasis should be placed on the horse's going well and willingly at his natural speed, and quality of riding should also come well into the picture. Dressage tests would then have far more meaning and purpose than they have now.

A warm-up routine

A properly carried out, effective warm-up and working-in session should also be performed before every lesson or hack so that the horse's body is loosened up and the blood flows delivering oxygen and nutrients – the supplies the body needs to perform the work to come with minimal risk of injury – and also to carry away the resultant waste products. The routine suggested below gives enough time not only to warm and loosen up the horse's body but also to get his mind working and responsive. It will wake him up if he is the sluggish type, get the itch out of his heels if he is a bit fresh and will discourage antics on the road if you are going for a hack.

Cold, stiff muscles, soft tissues and joints which are suddenly subjected to effort, sustain minor strain injuries, particularly in stabled horses who, quite unnaturally, spend most of their time stationary and not using their bodies, and these can build up into significant problems. But so many riders come into the arena 'on a contact' from the beginning, walk only one or two circuits and then go into a fast, demanding trot, normally with too heavy a contact because they think it is time to 'get the horse on the bit'; they are stiff and busy and tend to hold their horses up and in from the front with the reins, often supplemented by gadgets. I note that they also often look hard and serious, glare at the backs of their horses' heads (which, believe it or not, the horses do pick up) and do not appear to enjoy what they are doing at all. Their helpless horses adopt an equally stiff way of going, defending their bodies from the discomfort.

They often go faster and faster, and pull and resist or evade more and more, because they do not know what else to do or how else to cope with the discomfort, and are desperately trying to do what they think is required, or even just work out what that is.

This is not schooling or warming up. It is not even beneficial exercising but is a form of abuse, in my view. It can be injurious to the horse's body and mind and will certainly teach him various resistances which can result in incorrect muscle development and ways of going, and in stiffness and insidious strains which can progress to actual injuries. This sort of treatment also makes horses defensive or resentful, depending on their temperament, and can be the cause of unwillingness and active resistance, sometimes quite violent. This is surely no way to develop a good relationship with a horse or to get him to work well for the rider, which are the whole objects of riding or owning horses.

I offer the following as a good, planned warm-up routine which is easy to do and very effective. It uses gentle, non-demanding walking, trotting and cantering on each rein. Let the horse go in his natural way, on a long rein with just a light 'I'm here' contact on the bit and at a comfortable, *steady* speed. There is no effort to get him in hand and working at this stage. Keep yourself balanced and centred on his back with the vertical mid-line of your body lined up with the crest of his neck, look ahead through his ears, relax (particularly in the seat and legs) and do as little as you can whilst moving with the horse's movements.

Start on the horse's best rein and walk one circuit of the arena (assuming the average size of 20 m x 40 m and then walk a figure of eight consisting of two 20 m circles. Change over and do the same on his less good rein. Change again to his best rein and repeat the procedure in a *steady* trot, on both reins. Change the rein in walk; then, on his best rein, do the same thing in canter, coming down to trot or walk to change legs in the figure of eight, and also to change the rein on to his less good rein, on which you repeat the process one last time. Then come down to walk around on a loose rein (on the buckle) to let him

catch his breath before starting work or going out for a hack.

With a horse who is pretty fresh, in the canter period try cantering on *steadily* till he offers to stop or you feel he is thinking about it, then gently push him on for just one more circuit before coming down to a walk for a while. Then repeat this on the other rein, again doing just one more circuit than he really wants to do, and this should settle him enough to work safely and more sensibly.

This simple programme gives the horse enough chance to loosen and warm up (unless the weather is very cold in which case it can be extended) and it lets you feel him on the straight, on bends, in every gait and on both reins. It gives you plenty of chance to spot any problems such as resistance (for which there is always a reason), stiffness or lameness, which might be exacerbated if you started more demanding work before he was ready or before you had assessed him in all four points. Provided you feel he is loosened up and ready to respond, gradually start working and obtain some good, basic results in walk before moving on. At the end of the session, cool down by walking on a long or loose rein for about ten minutes.

Time for a break

When horses are asked to work within a gait at a speed faster – *or slower* – than their natural cruising speed, their energy use shoots up and the gait becomes uneconomical. I described earlier how horses have a natural, individual cruising speed within each gait, at which they feel most comfortable and move most efficiently with the least expenditure of energy and, therefore, the least need to increase their heart and breathing rates. It should be borne in mind that dressage horses, in particular, or horses doing a good deal of flatwork, spend much of their time working at speeds either side of their natural cruising speeds and therefore use up a lot of energy and are working harder than we may realise. They may also feel somewhat stressed out mentally because of this. If we understand this and give them shorter stints of work, letting them walk on a loose rein say every five minutes or so, even just for one circuit of the school or its equivalent, to relax their muscles and brains, we shall probably find that the tension decreases, their willingness and ability increase and their work improves.

Try holding your own body in an unnatural pose and moving that way for a full five minutes without relaxing, then try it for ten minutes, and then try to imagine how your horse must feel, particularly as he is not doing it voluntarily. Many people work their horses in so-called schooling sessions for much longer than this at a time. I have actually seen dressage riders who compete at quite a high level, and who really should know better, working horses for a full forty-five minutes with hardly a break. Muscles need to relax very frequently to keep the circulation going through them effectively.

If a muscle becomes tight or goes into spasm due to incorrect work and insufficient relaxation, it is obviously shortened and this places a more or less constant pull on its tendons and, through them, on the associated joints and ligaments. This can over-stress the whole body because the muscle system is closely integrated, stiffness and pain in one part often resulting in stiffness and pain elsewhere. The legs and back are the parts most affected and may start to suffer unexplained injuries which become chronic; these reduce a horse's quality of performance and can shorten his working life.

When a horse works correctly, his slightly convex shape is supported by his abdominal muscles which, basically, are attached to the underneath of the hind part of the spine, to the lower part of the pelvis, to the ribs and to the sternum or breastbone. When these all contract in work, so that the horse is going in a slightly humpty-backed posture, the slight arch of the spine is supported, the pelvis and thigh bones are tilted under the body and the whole under line or belly is shortened whereas the top line is gently stretched and lengthened. This makes for an effective, safer way for the horse to work whilst counteracting the forces placed on his body through making considerable physical efforts to carry or push weight.

The gaits

Walk, trot and canter are quite unlike each other but the gallop is simply a stretched out, faster version of the canter with no marked transition between the two, unlike the other gaits. Some horses also perform extra gaits, some of which are termed artificial but which appear natural to some horses, and there are also learned gaits which man teaches horses for his own purposes. In the natural category are the amble and its fast derivative, the pace, also the characteristic gait of the Icelandic Horse, the tølt. Learned gaits include the running walk, the stepping pace, the foxtrot and the rack or single-foot. These gaits, even the learned ones, can be enhanced in stock by being selected for. Horses with known abilities to perform them are mated together so that these abilities come out in their offspring and it is entertaining to watch young foals performing their natural version of an 'artificial' gait such as the pace in the field, keeping up with their dams.

Unfortunately for the student of conformation, there is no way that we can tell just by looking at a horse's make and shape which of these gaits he can perform. One has to see him in action and, in order to discover which gaits are natural to him, watch him at liberty or worked loose so that one can see what gaits he picks up from choice. Some individuals do have a natural inclination to move in particular gaits of their own volition although very few, in my experience, adopt learned gaits when moving at liberty.

The walk
This is the horse's slowest gait. Unless he is standing in an unbalanced way, he will nearly always start a stride (one sequence of four footfalls) with a hindleg. He moves both legs on one side first, then both legs on the other. In walk, then, the sequence will be, say, near hind, near fore, off hind, off fore. The walk is classed as a four-time, lateral gait because of the hoofbeats and the fact that both legs on one side move one after the other, then the legs on the other side. Many trainers demand that the horse performs a

strict march-type walk with no break between the footfalls on one side; for example, one, two, three, four, not one, two – three, four. In practice, a march walk is unnatural to many horses and a slight hiatus between the two pairs of lateral legs is normal – it is not a sign of laziness or of the horse not working properly. Horses with longish backs can find a march walk difficult and uncomfortable unless they are exceptionally well conformed in other ways and with free, scopey limb movement.

There are always at least two, and usually three feet on the ground in walk whereas in trot, canter and gallop there is a period when no feet are touching the ground and the horse is 'flying' through the air. This is called the 'moment of suspension'.

A good walk is said to be signified by the horse's over-tracking or placing his hindfoot well in front of the print just made by the forefoot on the same side. The distance varies according to the horse's size and conformation but in an average riding horse (if there is such a thing) an overlap of about 15 cm (6 in) is considered quite good.

The rein-back

The rein-back is interesting because horses do it naturally when manoeuvring their bodies, but only for a very few steps; then they usually turn to one side or the other and move forward in another gait. We think of it as a backward walk but it is actually a two-time diagonal gait because the horse moves diagonal pairs of legs (as in trot, which is why I have placed it between walk and trot) at the same time. Reining back is quite hard work and it is generally regarded as unfair to ask for more than six steps from even the best-suppled and muscled-up dressage horse, but it is also excellent for showing up back and hindleg weaknesses and lamenesses.

A horse with good overall balanced conformation, like this, should be able to move well in any gait but the proof of the pudding is always in the eating. This horse has a rather low set tail but, for jumping at least, it is better this way than the reverse. Normally, a well-set tail would be about level with the back

The trot

The trot is a two-time gait and is also called a diagonal gait. The horse moves his legs in alternate diagonal pairs; for instance, he will move the near hind and off fore forward together through the air, land on them, spring off the ground into a moment of suspension during which the other diagonal pair, the off hind and near fore, come forward and land, and so on. In this way, the horse is repeatedly springing from one diagonal pair of legs to the other, changing from one to the other in the air. Obviously, in the moment of suspension all four feet are off the ground and there are only ever two feet on the ground at the same time.

The trot can be performed on the spot (when it is a piaffe, formal or impromptu), in one of several ways moving forward (natural, working, medium, collected, passage and extended) and, the fastest way of all, the racing trot, in which the horse is fully extended with an elevated period of extension. Experts and purists have argued for decades, and probably centuries, about whether or not the period of suspension in the passage (the slowest but loftiest trot) is longer, giving the horse his appearance of dancing in air, or whether he spends longer on the ground with his hind joints well flexed to produce the spring.

The canter

The horse will begin a canter stride with a hindleg, say the near hind, bringing it forward and hitting the ground with it, then a diagonal pair of legs (in this case the off hind and near fore together) will come forward and hit the ground with both feet at the same time (in a correct, natural canter), then the off fore will come forward and hit the ground. This makes three beats audible so the canter is called a three-time gait. After the off fore leaves the ground, there is a moment of suspension during which the four legs are gathered together under the horse, then the near hind again comes forward to start the next stride. The horse can, similarly, start his stride with his off hind, then land the diagonal pair of near hind and off fore and finally the near fore.

It is rather silly to say that the foreleg which hits the ground alone and *last*, at the end of one stride, is the *leading* foreleg, but that is what we do because it looks to the human eye as though the horse is stretching out that leg in front of all the others – which I suppose he is. We say, then, that the horse is cantering with the near fore or the off fore leading, as the case may be.

If some horses are asked for a collected canter when they are not strong enough or schooled enough, are over-collected or not going properly, or are feeling pain or discomfort often in the back or hindlegs, they may produce a four-beat canter gait – say, near hind, off hind, near fore, off fore or vice versa. This is not natural and is not regarded as correct in schooling work or competition.

The gallop

This is a faster, stretched-out, four-time version of the canter, in which the horse begins a stride with a hindleg, followed by the other hindleg, then the two forelegs in the same order – for example, near hind, off hind, near fore, off fore. Then there is the moment of suspension. As with the canter, he can begin a stride with either hindleg and can lead at the gallop with either foreleg. The result is a very fast, regular, four-beat gait which novices find surprisingly easy, if somewhat frightening, to sit on.

The moment of suspension, as in canter, sees the horse with all his feet under his body but for hundreds of years this was not recognised. Because the horse's true movements are very difficult and at times impossible for the human eye to discern accurately, even the most highly respected horsemen, farriers (who then acted as the equivalent of vets as well) and artists believed that the horse had all his legs stretched out during the moment of suspension, like a cheetah, as shown by old paintings even by experts such as Stubbs. But thanks to the invention of photography and the famous gait analyses by Edward Muybridge, it was finally discovered that the exact opposite is the case. The most spectacular extension in fact occurs when the first (not leading) foreleg is about to hit the ground and this seems to be the image of a galloping horse which stays with the human eye and brain.

The gallop is faster than the canter because the horse never has more than two legs on the ground at once and can create a longer space between footfalls because of this. The canter is a steadier gait capable of being lengthened, shortened, collected and extended, although it must always remain a three-time gait, whereas the gallop is a definite four-time gait which can be either fast, faster or out of sight!

Speed in the horse is a topic somewhat outside the scope of this book, but it is interesting to note that a galloping equid (not only horses) can reach speeds of up to around 65 k.p.h. (40 m.p.h). However, harness racers (in both trot and pace, which is slightly faster than trot) and ridden trotters, not to mention the Icelandic Horse in his natural tølt, can reach speeds that are only slightly slower than this. The horse needs this speed at gallop for survival and for a big, heavy animal (the average riding horse weighs around 500 kg or 1/2 ton) it is an excellent speed. As we have seen, to prevent injury the back is held fairly rigid at fast speeds; most of the movement takes place in the neck vertebrae and at the lumbo-sacral joint which flexes up and down to permit the sacrum, the lower part of the pelvis and the thighbones to be tilted forwards under the body and the hindlegs to reach forwards under the horse in as long a stride as he is capable of at top speed. It is the lack of flexibility in the back which prevents him going faster because it limits him to one period of suspension in his gallop stride, after the leading foreleg lifts off.

Fortunately for wild and feral equidae (asses and zebras as well as horses), their most usual, feline predators have a similar top speed, which means that, so long as the equines as a herd remain alert, they can sense a predator's presence and get off to a good start. Running at about the same speed, they have a very good chance of staying ahead and alive. Whenever a foot hits the ground, the forward impetus is blocked and the horse is slowed down; therefore, the more time the horse can spend in the air the faster he will be.

Racehorses' top speeds are not increasing nearly so fast as they did during the last two centuries, and in most situations are not increasing at all. However, one reason for this is that horses do not race on such hard, 'fast' surfaces as they did generations ago. Nowadays, turf courses are watered and dirt courses harrowed, and the softer the going, even when classed as 'good', the slower horses run.

The pace

This is the fastest gait for harness racers and is a two-time lateral gait. The horse moves both legs on one side forward together and, as in trot, the feet hit the ground together – near hind and near fore, say, then off hind and off fore, hence its classification. To the uninitiated, the pace looks very like the trot with its determined one, two, one, two beat, but closer scrutiny reveals the lateral nature of this gait. Although it is defined as an artificial gait, some horses and ponies do pace naturally from foalhood, but when it comes to racing pacers, despite the horse's natural inclination, training and special harness are necessary because if the horse breaks gait he is disqualified. The fast, racing pace also has the disadvantage that if the horse does break gait into canter he cannot get back into pace but trots instead. Carefully adjusted hobbles (or hopples) in the form of long loops around each lateral pair of legs act as a strong encouragement to the horse to remain in pace.

Racing pacers are almost always faster than racing trotters (and can reach almost the same speed as galloping Thoroughbreds). This is because the period of suspension, when the horse is travelling through the air without restriction from the ground, is slightly longer in the pace than in the trot. In pace, the spine does not flex laterally as much as in trot but moves in more of a tilt or rotation from side to side. This results in more weight being thrown onto the legs as each lateral pair lands and so the fast pace is more stressful for the horse than the fast trot. Pacers can certainly be ridden but the fast pace usually feels rough under saddle, giving the rider an uncomfortable, rolling, side-to-side motion.

The amble

This is the gait from which the fast, racing pace developed. Unlike the racing pace, the slower but quite speedy amble is extremely smooth and comfortable for the rider and amblers were in great demand a few centuries ago when riding was the only real way to cover long distances with any ease and speed, that is, before roads improved enough for wheeled vehicles to be used.

The amble is a four-time lateral gait, like the walk – near hind, near fore, off hind, off fore – and also has no moment of suspension, but its rhythm is faster and its style, with the back remaining level with a gentle side-to-side rock, make it an obvious forerunner to the pace. There is a very slight pause between the two lateral pairs of legs hitting the ground, giving a rapid one, two – one, two time. The amble can be performed quite fast and can, unusually, be

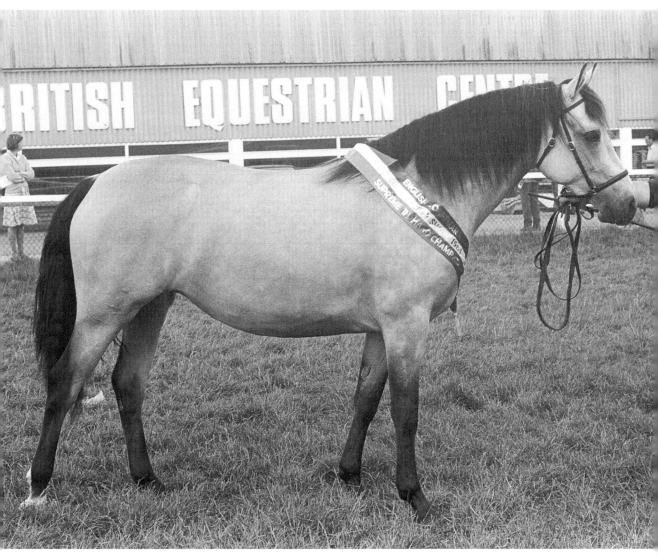

A champion Connemara filly of excellent conformation. Her loins and quarters, where the power for action comes from, are particularly eye-catching

executed in collection. In formal dressage, however, it is regarded as a serious gait defect. Having said that, some tired horses naturally revert to the amble for relief. The fact that the gait was popular for covering long distances in the days of ridden transport, that many horses have an inborn inclination towards it and that tired horses often do it, somewhat belies the belief that it is a very tiring gait. If only we could ask the horses. The better riders and trainers all stipulate that horses should not be held in any amble or similar gait, and particularly not in the single-foot or fast rack (see next section) for very long, but must be rested by being allowed to

perform a quite different gait using different muscles and placing different stresses on the body.

Some people demand that the amble must be performed in two-time, like a slow pace, and regard the four-time amble as a 'broken amble', the formal name for which is single-foot.

Single-foot

The single-foot, also called the rack or fast rack, is a fast, extravagant, four-time, gait used for display which is very popular in North American showing circles, and is performed by certain breeds (see Chapter 7) known as

This is a champion riding pony of Welsh/Arab/Thoroughbred breeding. Being somewhat croup-high, he would need to be put to mares who had no inclination in this respect, and would make a suitable sire for children's riding ponies and, on Thoroughbred mares, of show hacks and riding horses

five-gaited horses. It is called the single-foot because one foot hits the ground at a time.

In the fast rack, the horse slightly lowers his body, keeps his head still and moves his legs in a flashy, high gait which is exaggerated by training and ankle chains plus elongated feet and special shoeing, which encourage the horse to lift his feet high.

Years ago, I was speaking to a group of American veterinarians at a veterinary conference and they all agreed that, of all the artificial gaits, the fast rack in particular can cause considerable distress and back problems if badly ridden, particularly as many riders pull the horse's head up and back in a high but forced carriage, which kinks the neck in front of the withers, flattens the spine downwardly concave (with all the problems that brings about) and makes it impossible for the horse to bring his hindlegs underneath him properly. This is made even more difficult for the horse because most riders use saddles which deliberately place the rider behind the horse's centre of gravity, almost on the loins.

Well ridden, with the rider sitting in a seat which is less stressful for the horse, and with the head and neck carried voluntarily up and forward, also enabling the hindquarters and legs to do their job better, the fast rack can be a very impressive gait.

The tølt

This is the natural fast rack of the Icelandic Horse mentioned earlier but is performed without the exaggerated action of the fast rack and with the feet left in a natural state or shod normally. It is a very fast, four-time, lateral running walk with a strict, even one, two, one, two rhythm to which the rider can just sit and easily balance. There are tølt races in Iceland which are very exciting and popular. The small Icelandic Horses can reach speeds around 56 k.p.h. (35 m.p.h.) with ease.

Running walk and stepping pace

These so-called slow gaits are very similar to each other. They are four-time, lateral gaits which are very similar to the amble but performed with more brilliance.

The fox-trot

Officially described as a 'slow, shuffling trot', the fox-trot is the forte of the Missouri Fox Trotter. The gait is a short-striding one, and the horse actually walks with his front feet but trots with the hind, which step into the fore prints and then slide forwards, making for a very smooth gait to ride. The horse nods his head and clicks his front teeth together in time with his hoofbeats. This is obviously an artificial gait requiring training. The sequence of footfalls is, near hind, off fore, then a short pause, then off hind, near fore. The gait is, therefore, described as a four-time diagonal one. The fox-trot is said to be not as tiring for the horse as the amble or pace-related gaits and he can maintain it for long distances.

Gaited horses

In North American show rings, five-gaited horse classes are extremely popular and can be found in pockets in other countries, notably Australia and to a much lesser extent Great Britain.

Three-gaited horses present the normal walk, trot and canter. Five-gaited horses must present walk, trot and canter plus the fast rack and one of the slow gaits. The Tennessee Walker (formerly called the Plantation Walking Horse), however, is required to present the walk, a slow gait and the canter, being excused the trot.

Although the acquired or enhanced gaits can be fascinating to watch, it should be emphasised that they are part of a specialised segment of the horse world which most of the rest of us do not know enough about. As far as the Olympic and World Championship equestrian disciplines go, and the pleasure riding, hacking, showing and Riding Club events which concern most 'ordinary' riders, the four gaits which are important are the walk, trot, canter and gallop.

The gaits in action

The horse's way of going has been minutely honed over millions of years and his conformation is geared in synchrony with it. It is a very efficient method of motion for a four-legged animal of his make and shape.

We ask our equine athletes to perform physical feats far and above anything they would do in nature as far as combined speed, weight-carrying, jumping and stamina are concerned. Wild and feral equidae do travel over long distances, but at their own speed and comfortably within themselves. The only time they exert themselves significantly is when they are being chased by a predator or another horse who is being aggressive.

From a sports point of view, the horse is under significant stress much of the time when competing and training. Therefore, any deviation from perfection in both conformation and action can easily result in physical injury. As I have said, there is no such thing as a perfect horse, but many of the best performers in any field are extremely hard to fault and it is these that students of conformation and action should be watching and studying at every opportunity to get the picture they present ingrained into their subconscious. Any animal which consistently wins and performs well in active competition is worth studying. Show-ring competitors are not such a reliable subject for study, particularly in-hand (at-halter) entrants, as fashion in some breeds and types may produce animals which are not at all like the old, laid-down standards of their breed's or type's conformation and way of going. My personal view is to study *performers* – horses who have proved by tough competition that they have what it takes both to look good and to work well to a high standard.

A horse can adapt and compensate consciously for faulty conformation and action by moving differently from normal so as to reduce stress, discomfort and pain. His body also can compensate, by thickening a bone here, developing a muscle there and so on. When looking for a performance horse, though, it is safest to seek as near perfection as you can find. If the horse has a crooked action, puts a leg down crookedly, dishes, plaits, wings, brushes and so on, he is not only wasting energy carrying the leg out of its true, straight path but overloading some part of the limb and the body further up. The horse's legs should be straight from the point of view of action, as nature intended it; anything which deviates from this is a clear disadvantage.

For example, if a horse habitually puts his off fore down on the outside bearing surface first, then for an instant during every stride with that leg the outside bearing surface alone is taking all the weight which should be shared by the whole bearing surface, and this is more than nature intended it to take. The leg and body sense that they are being overstressed and try to compensate by producing more horn on the offside quarter and heel of the hoof, more or denser, stronger bone up the outside of the off foreleg, stronger soft tissues to take the extra stress, and so on. If this does not happen, or if the precise action and weight-bearing function is too much for the horse's make and shape, injury can occur. The bone is constantly slightly compressed by the excess weight up that side of the leg and on the inside of the leg there may be some stretching of the soft tissues causing soft tissue injury involving ligaments, connective tissue, muscles or tendons as the weight finally falls on to the left side of the bearing surface and on up the leg, once the foot is on the ground.

This is only one example but I hope it shows how important even natural compensatory stresses are in exaggerated conditions such as the extreme performance work of the equine athlete. Even exceptionally well-conformed, trained and managed horses are not guaranteed to stay sound when placed under severe stress. The body can only take so much over and above nature's limits.

When considering a horse's movement, it should be borne in mind that action can be improved by means of correct gymnastic schooling and good farriery, but no one can make a silk purse out of a sow's ear.

Overall impression

The best way to judge a horse or pony's action initially is to see him at liberty in a large enough space for him to move freely, to get up some speed at some point, and to move fairly naturally. The ideal is an undulating field so that you can check how he handles himself on the flat, up and down slopes and over uneven ground. The second best option, because restricted spaces always inhibit a horse's action, is for him to be at liberty in a smaller outdoor paddock, an outdoor school or an indoor *manège*, and the third best is to have the horse stood up in hand, then walked out and trotted up. Placing a rider on his back will *always* alter his natural action.

Most sellers or people presenting horses for assessment will automatically stand, walk and trot up the horse in hand first, so you will probably have to request to see the horse free. When you do see him led up in hand, make absolutely sure that the handler lets him go on a completely loose rein or rope, as even a slight tension on the headcollar or bridle can affect his action. Even just wearing a headcollar can inhibit some horses because of the psychological restraint it represents. Definitely do not accept a run-up with the handler hanging on to the horse's head, as this can very significantly disguise his action for better or for worse, pull him off line so that his legs, head and neck, and the rest of his body, swing about, and even give some support to a lame or stiff horse or a bad mover. Seeing a horse presented on the lunge and sent on too much with the whip can also give a false impression of his action, so ask for the process to be kept fairly casual.

The main quality to look for in an equine performer in any discipline, and the first impression you should get when assessing a horse for general ease and quality of movement, is a loose, easy, fluid and mobile body, with the horse appearing confident and looking as though he knows where he is going. Each gait should show regularity and symmetry – an even rhythm and even-length strides on both reins and in all gaits. However, as most horses have a preference, however slight, for one rein rather than the other, in the same way that humans are right- or left-handed, a *slight* difference is normal, even in a trained horse.

The walk

The horse needs a long-striding walk, with the back and tail swinging, and most observers also look for a horse who overtracks well in walk and tracks up or overtracks in trot; however, much depends on the horse's natural build, the

freedom of his joints, particularly at elbow and stifle, the length of his back, the angles of his hind limbs, shoulder and elbow (the slant of the humerus) and the length of his legs. If the horse does not actually overtrack, it is not necessarily a bad sign. In walk, a good length of overtrack should be around 15 cm (6 in), but I have studied some of the best racehorses in the world who overtracked by twice that much, and this applies to other disciplines, too, particularly hunters intended for galloping country and also event horses. These horses were all 16 hands high or over, so allowances must be made for an individual's height and also the length of his legs and back.

Check also that the horse is moving from his hips and shoulders, not merely from the stifle and elbow. His whole body should appear to move, not just his legs. Watch the shoulders and see the tops of the shoulder blades move backward and the bottoms of the shoulder blades (the points of the shoulders) move forward with each step, and try to spot the scapular fulcrum around which the shoulder blade rotates.

Watch the horse's hips and hindlegs and check that you can actually see movement in the femur (thigh bone), which is covered by muscle and which runs from the horse's stifle, sloping up and back to join the pelvis at the hip joint (not the point of hip). See how much forward movement you can detect in the stifle. The whole side of the horse's hindquarter should be seen to move forward; the leg should not move only from the stifle itself. If you imagine a straight vertical line dropped from the point of the hip (the wing of the pelvis) to the ground, watch to see how far in front of and behind that line the hindleg extends: the distance should be the same either side of the line – in other words, the leg should come as far in front of the line as behind it. In my experience, however, few horses manage this, often because of some physical problem which prevents engagement such as the saddle, the rider or an injury, but sometimes because of only moderate conformation as well. *This criterion can be applied to the trot too.*

The appearance should be of the horse's whole body moving fluidly and freely, shoulders and hips moving forward and backward with each step, his tail swinging, and his back and ribcage also swinging from side to side when viewed from slightly above and behind. The hips should rise and fall to even heights and the head and neck should swing slightly from side to side and up and down. If there is any apparent stiffness, rigidity, unevenness or reluctance to 'let go', suspect a problem.

There should be good hock flexion and movement in any breed or type, with the hindfeet landing about midway under the horse's belly. The forefeet should land under his head and his knee action should be commensurate with his breed and type. The hindlegs should follow the path of his forelegs, not deviating to either side, and the forelegs themselves should swing backward and forward in their single plane, also not deviating.

If you see all these general pointers in the walk, the 'Mother of All Gaits', you can be 90 per cent sure that the other gaits will be as good, although there are exceptions.

The trot

In trot, the horse should track up at least and ideally overtrack a little. The head and neck are comparatively still in trot but the horse should show no rigidity of movement in his body. He should swing along and spring freely from diagonal to diagonal. Again, there must be good hock flexion and movement, and thrust from the hindlegs. Remember to check how far in front of and behind a vertical line dropped from the point of hip the hindlegs extend – the distance should be equal.

As we have seen, a horse's conformation should be checked with him standing evenly and to attention on a level surface, but the next stage will be to ask for him to be walked and trotted up in hand. The walk gives a good idea of what the other gaits will be like but the trot is also excellent because it is the most symmetrical gait and even slight gait defects will be shown up.

It is the most useful gait for testing whether or not a horse is actually lame (or 'unlevel' or 'not right', which both mean 'lame'!) because it is faster than the walk and there is therefore more force generated on the legs. Moreover, the horse only has one other leg (on the opposite diagonal) to help share his bodyweight, unlike the walk where there are usually two other legs in support to lessen the weight on a lame leg. The horse will bear more weight on the leg which does not hurt and less on the painful leg and this produces an unevenness of action which does not occur in walk unless the horse is very lame. If he is trotted steadily in a circle (say, on a loose lunge rein) on a hard surface and on both reins, this will show up the tiniest gait defect and is a standard lameness test.

The canter

The canter should be naturally balanced and the horse should be seen to be driving from the back with his quarters working well, good leg extension and good stifle and hock flexion, ideally with an 'uphill' look to the body. Lameness is very difficult to detect in canter because of the nature of the gait and may only be obvious if the horse is very lame. If he is in pain anywhere, it is more likely to be shown by resistances and evasions.

The canter is the most important gait for a jumping horse of any discipline and should appear to be light, bouncing and effortless, with good natural balance. The horse should not be inclined to go on to his forehand when the speed is increased.

Anyone who has watched a horse canter free may have noticed that he often leads with the 'wrong' leg on gentle bends, and also leans in on tighter bends, carrying his head to the outside of the circle – all regarded as sins in dressage and general riding. But perhaps we should accept that the horse sometimes is the best judge of his own body and balance. In free, feral or wild conditions, horses do not canter for long distances even when migrating to a new area, and they frequently slow down or change direction, which enables them to change legs as they see fit – or they will walk for a while. Leaning in on sharpish bends ('motorbiking' to use a common term) with the head to the outside is the horse's natural way of balancing his large, heavy body with its fairly rigid spine in fast gaits to prevent him falling over. The reason we ask ridden horses not to do this is because if they did our extra weight on top, also leaning in, might well tip the balance and the horse could lose his footing. It is also not a reassuring way of going for a rider to experience. However, we should consider that we are placing an artificial stress on our horses in asking them to go 'upright' round tight bends with their heads to the inside of the circle. When looking for an athletic performer, then, look for a free horse who leads with what we consider to be the 'correct' leg and who looks where he is going, but the head may turn to the outside on a sharp turn.

The performance of counter-canter, in which the horse travels, say, on the right rein but in position left (with the near fore leading and flexed to the left) is a gymnastic exercise aimed at increasing suppleness and co-operation. Horses themselves may do it when free, but certainly not on sharp bends at any speed, when they will lead with the foreleg on the side towards which they are going, albeit with the head often to the opposite side for balance.

Flying changes, as we call changes of leg at the canter, are not particularly complicated for a horse to do on his own (day-old foals can do them) but they can become an advanced movement with a rider on top. It is a natural movement for the horse and experienced showjumpers do it all the time without being asked, in order to keep their balance during changes of direction between fences. I was once speaking to an international showjumping rider who said he had no idea how to get his horse to do a flying change other than by 'throwing myself to the other side'; if the horse could not do it on his own, and know when to do it (including during the flight phase of a jump), he would not last long in his yard. Horses should always be able to perform effortless flying changes at liberty. If they cannot or habitually come down for a stride or two of trot before cantering on the other leg, there could be a problem with natural balance and co-ordination.

Particularly in dressage and showjumping, this is cause for concern.

If a horse is lame, it is understandable that he will not want to lead at canter with a lame foreleg or strike off with a lame hind one (which initiates the stride), because it will be the sole leg in support, taking all his weight and maybe that of a rider, and will hurt. Therefore, a reluctance to take up a particular lead should set alarm bells ringing.

The gallop

Horses intended for galloping should be well balanced and able to extend well with impressive ground-covering strides. The hindquarters should flex notably from the lumbo-sacral joint, tilting the lower part of the pelvis down and forward under the horse and taking the thigh bones with it so that the horse reaches well under the body with his hindlegs and produces a noticeable strong thrust backward over the maximum distance. The shoulders should rotate freely and the forelegs should extend well with a reaching-out motion, not merely doing just enough to stop the horse falling on his nose.

Galloping horses are perfectly capable of doing flying changes at high speed; it is not an educated dressage movement but a perfectly natural one with a purpose, even on a straight line. Racehorses often do it for a change to rest tired muscles, but because horses are so sensitive to their own bodies, most will realise that, when being asked for more and more speed, changing legs actually produces a slight increase in speed for a second by reorganising the point at which a hindleg is planted forward on the ground to begin the next stride. Imagine in very slow motion that the near hind is due to be put down at the gallop to start a new stride (the off fore having just landed): it is coming forwards through the air but the horse decides to change legs and overtakes the near hind with his off hind, planting it several inches in front of where the near hind would have landed, so lengthening the distance during which he is in the air – the suspension phase – and 'hitching' the whole stride forward a little. Although tempi changes (changes of leg at every stride) at the gallop may not be wanted (although horses have been taught to do things just as artificial as that), perhaps racehorses could be taught to do flying changes when being pressed to or on the line and so gain vital inches.

The jump

Jumpers should have a natural way of snapping up their forelegs from the elbows and folding fully at the knees, as well as tucking up (fully flexing) their hindlegs. They should use their heads and necks, their built-in balancing poles, to the full (so it is best to watch them jump loose so that there can be no rider interference) and really reach out and down over their fences. Movements such as twisting over the obstacle, kicking out with the hindlegs, hesitating over a small fence or charging off or bucking on landing can indicate reluctance and pain, often in the back or forefeet or legs.

A good way to check the jumping potential of a young, possibly unbacked, horse is to watch him jumping free. A very few horses will deliberately jump obstacles in the field for fun. If they do, it is a good indicator of both physical and mental propensity but failing this, have the horse jumped loose in a prepared area, preferably loose in a *couloir* or jumping lane, indoors or out. Unhindered by human restraint, he should naturally lengthen his stride coming into the fence, decelerate in the final stride, lower his chest slightly to the ground approaching take-off, bring his hindlegs under and lower and lengthen the head and neck. The hindlegs propel the horse over the fence and the usual advice is to look for a horse which bascules over the fence (makes an arc with its body). This is actually an optical illusion created by a horse who stretches its head and neck well out and down over the fence during the flight phase. The spine actually remains straight and quite rigid which, in such a heavy animal, is necessary for lifting thrust and to prevent injury. The highest point of the horse when rising over the fence should be the withers, certainly not the poll.

The horse should not be excessively encouraged by ground helpers, particularly by means of the lungeing whip, but should show his own willingness and confidence. He should be able to tackle a reasonable fence without slowing down, making a big job of organising himself before take-off or charging off too fast after landing. Allowance should be made for young horses who dangle their legs somewhat over fences – something which more schooled horses must not do. It is more important generally to test a youngster's style and attitude than his aptitude for clearing heights and spreads.

Balance and co-ordination

You can certainly check this whilst the horse is at liberty or being ridden by other riders, but the acid test, if you are a good rider yourself, is to test it by riding him on a long to loose rein in a similar routine to the warm-up session described on page 93 – on both reins, on circles, round bends, with frequent changes of direction and pace within a gait and in all gaits but, particularly for performance horses, in canter, as most of them are required to jump in one discipline or another, competitive or otherwise.

The horse should easily accommodate himself to your requests and should find it easy to go round generous curves (above 15 m circles) flexed to the inside and without motorbiking. Resistance on smallish circles (12–15 m or less) indicates a problem for a supposedly finished or fairly well-schooled horse although green horses may experience a problem. A finished horse must be able to execute 10 m circles effortlessly and correctly on a loose rein under a good rider.

The hindfeet must always follow in the track of the forefeet, except when performing lateral work, the horse should maintain the gait requested by the rider and his gaits must retain their true footfall: disunited or 'broken' gaits, particularly a disunited canter (in the U.S.A. a round gallop) are anathema to the athletic equine. (In a disunited canter the footfalls are, for example, off hind, near hind, near fore, off fore. This places a great deal of stress on the horse's hips, spine, shoulders and legs and there is no place in athletic pursuits for a horse who is inclined to break into this false gait.)

Other faults such as the horse appearing to 'hold' himself in a defensive posture, cramped, shortened strides or a rolling action are also bad *especially in a free horse*. Many people are unaware of the effects that even wearing a saddle, let alone having a rider in it, have on a horse's action; even a mildly uncomfortable or irritating saddle or girth will shorten the gait or irregularise it, so do ask to see the horse moving ideally with no tack at all on him to get a clear impression. If the gait worsens much under saddle it will probably be the fault of either the rider or the tack, or both.

A well-balanced, comfortably moving horse in walk can be heard to place more weight or emphasis on his hindfeet than his fore. If we regard the sequence of walk, a lateral gait, as hind, fore, hind, fore, the footfalls should sound like *hind*, fore, *hind*, fore, not hind, *fore*, hind, *fore*.

How the horse jumps

Good jumping trainers encourage their students to adopt the attitude that a fence is simply a minor obstacle to the track, the exact route that they have planned to ride round the course. 'Ride your track,' is often the advice, 'the jump is just a slight obstacle in the way and won't interrupt the flow.' Brilliant if you can do it! But is it true? Let us take a look at just what horses do with their bodies when they jump a fence, and see whether a jump is merely an extension of a normal canter stride or not. From my personal experience and from interviews and observations at all levels, very, very few riders find it easy to almost disregard a fence and think of it as a 'slight obstacle in the way'!

There are five phases to jumping any obstacle: the approach, the take-off, the flight, the landing and the getaway. Let us imagine a showjumper performing in the most usual gait of canter, bearing in mind that horses can jump out of any gait from stop to gallop.

In the approach, the horse will be in canter, using the normal sequence. He will lower his body in the last few strides of the approach. In the last stride before take-off, he 'props' somewhat with his forelegs and decelerates sharply, so the ground represents a significant braking influence and interruption to the stride flow. His hindfeet break the normal sequence and swing forward, ideally exactly together, planting on the ground side by side under the body, forward of the position just vacated by the forefeet. He assumes a half-sitting posture which deeply flexes and engages the hindlegs and quarters well under the body, and his head and neck lower.

In the take-off, all the hindleg joints are flexed as the horse prepares to push his half-ton weight against the force of gravity. His torso rises in front of the fence and his head and neck swing up and back to assist this action. The shoulders rotate to bring the forelegs up in a flexed posture. The hindlegs, from being deeply flexed, rapidly straighten out and thrust the horse's body up and forward over the fence.

In the flight phase, the hind limbs have fully extended to drive the horse up and forward over the fence and the hindfeet have left the ground, so the horse is completely off the ground. The hindlegs begin to flex again once the horse is over the fence to clear the obstacle, the head and neck stretch forward and downward, balancing the body, and the forelegs also tuck up. Four well-tucked legs are the sign of an educated, experienced jumper trying his best not to touch his fence although some horses, particularly over spread fences, extend their legs right out in front of them.

The trajectory or parabola the body follows in the air depends entirely on the angle at which the horse thrusts himself off in take-off and that at which gravity brings him down again.

As the horse begins to come down from the maximum height of his flight, his hindlegs stay tucked up and his forelegs begin to unfold and extend ready to take his entire weight in the *landing* phase. The head and neck swing up and back, which not only helps to balance the horse but also helps to reduce the tremendous weight and force to be taken on first one foreleg then the other as the horse lands. This action also helps to transfer the almost vertical direction of the landing into the horizontal one he will assume when he gets away after his jump.

In the landing, one fore hoof will hit the ground first followed quickly by the next landing in front of it. This moving-on action of first one foot taking the strain then the other greatly helps to reduce the force of the landing, but the horse's body nevertheless experiences a considerable braking force. The fetlocks will flex to their fullest as the joints, tendons and ligaments take the strain of the weight and force, the knees remain rigid to support the horse like the spokes of a wheel and experience a good deal of backward force against them, and the joints of the elbow and shoulder will flex to help absorb this force. The soft tissues of the thoracic sling will 'give' under the weight and greatly absorb jar.

The hindfeet land one after the other and trained, experienced jumpers can learn to minimise the sudden stopping effect of hitting the ground by bringing the hindfeet well forward. When horses tackle drop fences, they usually have to land with both forefeet at almost the same time, which is the most dangerous type of landing for them because there is no natural, flowing, forward movement to reduce the force. Instead, both fetlocks are deeply depressed to their maximum, the bones and cartilages of the knees are considerably compressed and the elbow and shoulder joints again take their maximum force. The back, too, can be jarred. Landing from a drop fence onto rising ground makes the strain on the tendons, fetlocks and feet even worse and should, in my view, not be allowed in competition (we are not at war, after all) and should also be avoided as far as possible in non-competitive situations such as hunting and training. The stresses and strains are reduced if the landing is on ground which slopes slightly down and away from the fence as this allows the body and legs to flow forward and downward with the impetus of their own effort and of gravity.

In the getaway, the hindlegs have rapidly come down under the horse, one quickly following the other, to take the weight of the descending hindquarters and thrust the body up and forward, freeing the forelegs to pick up and continue the stride. The head and neck again drop, the horse pushes forward with his hindlegs and

continues in a normal footfall sequence in the following stride.

You could therefore be excused for regarding a jump as considerably more than a 'slight obstacle' in your path, a minor interruption to your plans, but rather as something worthy of considerable respect! You are not alone – your horse will agree with you! However, jumping is also about confidence and the old adage about 'throwing your heart over the fence' is excellent advice, but outside the scope of this book.

The jumping action

In the early 1980s, Christopher Biddle MSc wrote a ground-breaking series for *Equi* magazine, which I was then publishing, entitled 'The Ability to Jump in Horses', which raised a good deal of controversy and discussion at the time. His original work and thinking was refreshing at a time when everyone was still in the habit of accepting received wisdom and teaching as correct. People are finally becoming more discerning, enquiring, questioning and open-minded, although we still have a long way to go.

One of the first things Biddle pointed out was that, in contrast to the cat and the dog, the horse's large and heavy herbivorous digestive system had, over the course of evolution, necessitated a strong and fairly rigid spine to support it and stressed: 'This is a real detriment to efficient jumping. A consequence of this spinal rigidity is that the horse is no longer [unlike its early ancestors] able to place its hind hoof beyond its own midpoint, thus its length of stride and potential to spring are greatly reduced.' (One reason deer, also herbivores, are such brilliant jumpers is that they are ruminants and so do not need the capacious, heavy hind gut of the horse. Cattle are also herbivores, of course, but have neither the make and shape nor the inclination for jumping.) Other points Biddle made were:

- The horse has had to develop a long neck and large, heavy head because of its diet, unlike the short necks and comparatively small heads of cats and dogs. Although the head and neck are useful as a balancing 'bob', they also add bulk and weight at the front end – an added problem in jumping larger obstacles.

- The horse's increased speed and endurance as survival mechanisms have resulted in the retention of only one toe on the end of the leg, which makes for lightness. The horse has also adopted an upright stature, unlike the more crouched, almost rabbit-like stance of *Hyracotherium*, and has developed long leg bones; although this allows for an increase in the length of his stride and speed, it prevents the horse being able to store potential energy to spring suddenly without much preparation.

- The loss of heavy, bulky muscles from the lower leg lightens the leg, allowing faster movement. Further enhancement of the horse's speed by attaching the muscles of the limbs close to the joints or fulcrum points of the limbs has enabled a small muscle movement there to become magnified into a large limb movement at the opposite ends of the bones. Although this increases the potential for speed, it means that the muscle is disadvantaged when asked to lift a half-ton horse over an obstacle of, say, 1.5 m (5 ft).

- The problem of speed versus power (the latter being the major component of jumping) is further stressed by the angle of insertion of the muscles which is very acute in the limbs of the horse, aiding speed but being mechanically disadvantageous for power. Increasing either the muscle size or the ratio of the bone of the lower limb to the upper limb are both mechanically disadvantageous. The first adds weight and the latter produces a longer stride which enhances speed, *neither of which assist the act of jumping.*

So how can the horse get over his inherent problems? Christopher Biddle found that human athletes use their toes a good deal in jumping and many expert horsemen and women felt that the rotation of the toe down and back was also responsible for the final push to propel the horse over an obstacle. However, he made a study of many photographs and slow-motion films of horses jumping and it became apparent to him that the toes are not used significantly but that much greater emphasis is placed on the action of the hocks and fetlocks.

He also observed at several indoor shows that the surface did not dig up in front of the fence, as would happen if toe propulsion were used, and that little or no material was kicked back at take-off, suggesting that the feet were planted squarely on the ground throughout that phase. When he continued the study on turf, his findings were confirmed by similar depth depressions for both toe and heel in the earth at take-off points.

When he examined the peculiar circumstance of the puissance parabola (the arc the horse describes over a very high fence), Biddle found, by taking photographs during competition and analysing heights and take-off distances afterwards, that extra height is not achieved by increased speed, as had always been believed, and that the ideal take-off point is a lot closer to the fence than its height. Positive forehand elevation must therefore occur by means of considerable use of the muscles of the abdomen, back and hindquarters in particular, a situation which had not, until that point, been appreciated.

The anatomy of a jumper

As part of his study, Biddle also compared the structure of international showjumpers with that of a 'normal' control group of horses. The subjects were grouped into unsuccessful horses and proven winners, with a small group of potential winners included. He made a particular examination of the current British High Jump Champion, Lastic, who was ridden by Nick Skelton.

The horses were photographed from identical positions and angles, a metre rule being incorporated to standardise all the photographs before analysing them. The results provided a 'close approximation of the skeletal levers using easily identifiable, recognisable and reproducible landmarks and thus consistency in results. The points chosen were those thought most suitable to demonstrate jumping abilities.'

Various measurements were taken and tabulated, then subjected to statistical analysis to identify any significant measurements. The mean and standard deviations were calculated, then subjected to the 't' test to establish true significance. The 't' test is a statistical test to show that the difference seen in samples could not have occurred by chance. It was decided, for this analysis, that a probability of the difference occurring by chance of less than 5 per cent was significant.

The international showjumpers in the experiment were about three years older than the control horses; this was felt to be roughly the time required to obtain the relevant experience. The following findings are a direct quotation from Christopher Biddle's series in *Equi*:

- The internationals were about 3 cm taller, which is only 1 per cent different significant at the 5 per cent level but not at the 2.5 per cent; *thus, height is necessary for a showjumper.*
- The length of the back is *not* significant at the 5 per cent level, which is *contrary to the opinion of experts that a good showjumper requires a short back*, while the length of the neck is significant to the 2.5 per cent, a factor seldom mentioned in the literature! *A longish neck is an advantage, therefore.*
- Head size was found to be the same for both [groups of horses] as were the knee-to-ergot, fetlock-to-ground and pelvic dimensions.
- The length of the elbow to knee differed by 1.5 per cent which was significant at the 2.5 per cent level, so *a long forearm is desirable.*
- The femur [thigh bone] was found to be similar as were the tuber calcis [point of hock bone], hind cannon, pastern and the circumference of girth, hocks and fetlocks – of no special significance.
- However, *the circumference of the knee was found to be significantly larger in the internationals*, while the equine terminology of 'bone' *viz.* cannon bone and associated tendons, was found *not* to be significant, which again is contrary to expert opinion which lays great emphasis on 'bone'.
- The most significant difference was, however, found in the *tibia which was found to be some 16 per cent larger in the internationals and, in fact,* *was 48 per cent larger in the British High Jump Champion, Lastic.*

Biddle concluded that of the twenty-two dimensions measured five were statistically significant, that is 22 per cent, while the remaining 78 per cent were within the normal population range, indicating that the two samples were reasonably similar.

So, then, if you are looking for a jumper in any discipline it would seem that you need to look for:

- height
- a longish neck
- a long forearm
- a large knee circumference
- a particularly long tibia (gaskin)

The advice to look for great length from point of hip to hock in a jumper could, in the light of the above research, be modified to recommend length from stifle to hock, which are the two points between which the gaskin runs.

You may wonder why I have included twenty-year-old research in this book. The reason is that, despite searching the literature, I have found nothing quite like Christopher Biddle's findings in the interval since its publication, although there is a good deal of research going on in North America. If anyone knows of any relevant work, or has done any themselves, I should be most interested to hear from them.

Piece by piece

Let us now look at various parts of the horse and at how their structure could affect his ability to do different sorts of work. It is a good idea to remember the basic blueprint outlined in Chapter 5 and the importance of overall balance and symmetry when considering individual parts in more detail.

The head and neck
It is common to hear the rather facetious remark that the head is not important in assessing

conformation because 'you don't ride the head'. But of course, the head *is* important, because its weight will affect the horse's balance, depending on the dimensions of the neck, the way the head is joined to it and the dimensions between the jawbones, which affect the horse's ability to 'bridle', flex, come 'on the bit', accept the bit and so on. Any horse that will not do those things (which are variations of the same thing) will never make a good riding horse. Stiffness in this, the throatlatch, area is reflected throughout the whole horse. If a rider is successful in persuading her horse to part the two jawbones slightly by dropping the lower jaw a little way, and *allowing* him to do so by having a loose enough noseband, it loosens the whole poll area because the lower jaw is joined to the upper jaw just below the ear. Tension here runs right down the muscles of the neck and shoulders, the back and the hindlegs, making it more or less impossible for the horse to engage behind and go in the posture described.

A wide throatlatch area is therefore a big advantage because it will allow the windpipe to pass through unhindered and provides plenty of room for the vital supply of oxygen. If you can fit two fingers' width between the top of the round jawbone and the top neck vertebra it probably means that the horse has a long poll with room to flex without painfully crushing the salivary glands situated in this region. A narrow throatlatch has all the opposite effects – insufficient room for the windpipe, with a possible reduction in airflow. A tight conformation between the head and the neck will make it uncomfortable or even painful for the horse to flex from the poll and is a frequent cause of horses flexing lower down the neck, which is incorrect and also inefficient from the point of view of correct use of the muscles of the neck and shoulders.

The shape of the nose or front line of the face is largely a matter of personal preference. It is found that in cold-blooded breeds and types of horse and pony the rounded, outwardly convex or Roman nose often regarded as ugly and common in riding breeds is a definite advantage because it provides plenty of space for warming

inhaled cold air in their natural environment. Many warmbloods and a few Thoroughbreds exhibit a tendency to this shape as a result of their mixed ancestry; the Thoroughbred has many unknowns, usually mares, in the very early years of its formation, and warmbloods are all descended from heavy horses.

A so-called 'dished' or inwardly concave front line of the face, particularly in modern Arabian horses, is often highly prized by their breeders and actively selected for in mating. However, it can be a big disadvantage in a performance animal if it is pronounced because it reduces the airspaces and passages in the head and could restrict the amount of air which it is possible for the horse to inhale, so reducing oxygen supply and performance ability. Exercise intolerance is the last thing you want in a performance horse and although many show-ring specimens have this conformation in the extreme, it is a dangerous point to breed for because it will filter out through the breed as a whole, to its detriment. The Arab was bred, above all, as an athletic warhorse and exaggerated qualities like this, which actually look ugly and deformed to many people who understand conformation, should be discouraged.

Whatever the shape of a horse's head, his nostrils should be large enough for his purposes. Any animal working at slow gaits, not working hard or living in a cold climate can manage perfectly well with small nostrils and the air-supply restrictions they bring, but others, particularly performance horses, need generous nostrils for obvious reasons.

The neck and head must look like a matched pair for efficiency of balance. There needs to be enough length in the neck for effective balance and the longer the neck than average the smaller the head should be, within reason. Heavy draught breeds of horse and pony can afford to have short, muscular, strong necks and fairly large heads which are fine for their work; indeed, long necks and big heads would put them at a disadvantage in terms of balance as they push forwards into their harnesses to move heavy weights. In fact, even in riding breeds, a short neck is less of a disadvantage than a long one, which can unbalance a horse if it has a big head on the end of it and is set low on the chest. Necks which come out of the chest low down or horizontally prevent the horse ever being really light in hand; indeed, such horses and ponies are usually very good pullers!

The term bull neck is applied to the very short, thick neck often found in heavy breeds, many cobs, heavy-type ponies and specific breeds of those types; even some Thoroughbred sprinters and Quarter Horses can be found with this neck conformation. To ride, bull-necked horses are often heavy in hand despite the fact that their necks are often high-set, and can pull for their lives – not a pleasant sensation. Such animals, however, take well to correctly performed neck reining in a sensitively-used curb-type bit, when it is impossible for them to pull. For driving, though not smart carriage driving, bull-necked horses are no disadvantage because they have plenty of muscle to activate the forelimbs but care needs to be taken in the fitting of the collar.

The ewe neck was described at some length in Chapter 1. The neck looks as though it was put on upside down and the head usually forms a right-angle to it at the throat, the whole combination making it impossible for the horse to really stretch his head and neck out and down properly and to flex adequately at the poll. It is the angle of the head which gives these horses their nickname of 'stargazers'.

Horses with this conformation often have a dip in front of the withers; they are 'kinked' there, which can tighten all the neck, shoulder, back, loin and hind-end muscles without any effort from the horse because of the tension. Such horses rarely look where they are going and can easily trip and fall, not least because of the lack of a proper way of going. The horse finds it extremely difficult to lower his head and neck, raise his withers, shoulders and back and lower his hindquarters into engagement

The combination can be improved by a competent, sensitive rider but these horses will never reach high performance levels, although that does not mean they will never win anything. Schooling over poles and grids will produce some improvement. Outline-fixing devices such as draw-reins or tight side-reins should not be used – at the most, a properly used chambon or maybe a de Gogue, or a Tellington body wrap.

Swan necked horses can look elegant to the uninformed observer but they do present problems. The main giveaway is a kink in front of the withers, combined with an attractive-looking arch further up which gives the impression that

A swan neck. This conformation often looks beautiful and elegant to the uninitiated but such horses often do not accept the bit and 'bridle' well and find it hard to go with their heads down and gently stretched in training, to enable the back to rise and the correct muscles to be developed

A bull neck. This conformation often results in horses which are heavy in hand and natural pullers and 'leaners'. Riding them correctly in a curb bit defeats this unpleasant performance fault

the horse can flex easily to the bit. Indeed he can, often to the extent of quickly learning the difficult-to-cure evasion of being behind the bit in heavy hands.

These horses usually have high-set necks and are not on the forehand, which makes them deceptively comfortable to ride; however, they tend not to work properly from behind and sail along looking pretty, giving uneducated riders the sensation that all is well. Then, because they are not engaged, if they spook the riders are faced with problems of control.

The same basic schooling – correct long-and-low work over poles encouraging hindquarter engagement – will improve the way of going of swan necked horses and get them between leg and hand.

The shoulder

Long, well-sloped, laid-back shoulders already described are preferred in most equestrian sporting disciplines. The approximate angle of the spine of the scapula with an imaginary horizontal line drawn alongside the horse's body is 45°. This sort of shoulder provides good absorption of concussion and, elbow permitting, allows the foreleg to extend well in front of the horse for maximum scope and the ability to rotate the shoulder and tuck up the forelegs when jumping. It also usually provides comfort in the ride and, as it often accompanies well-formed withers and a deep chest, the saddle is kept in place and the horse has a good capacity for air exchange. The length of the scapula allows plenty of room for muscle attachment and athletic performance and gives the rider the comforting feeling of having plenty in front.

An upright shoulder, on the other hand, is often restricted in action and can make for a jarring ride particularly if the horse also has upright pasterns. This type of shoulder often accompanies a ewe neck, short front and low withers. Even with an open elbow, the horse will take shortish strides and will never have the scope or suppleness for athletic activities. He will take more strides and so use up more energy, and he will subject his legs to concussion

and hence possibly not remain sound, even in moderate work.

However, it is found that quite a few horses in sprinting and quick-start activities are upright in the shoulder. This formation creates an obtuse angle of the point of shoulder/humerus joint which may make jumping difficult when it comes to lifting the forelegs but which makes the rapid striding which is advantageous for sprinting sports (racing, polo, cutting cattle) easier. Driving horses may also have upright shoulders as many people feel it is easier for them to push into the collar – although it must be said that others hold the opposite view.

A short humerus/upper arm bone is often found to be more horizontal than is normally desired, which reduces scope and jumping ability and produces a shortened stride, as the foreleg is usually set too far under the shoulder because of it. Such horses may be used for sprinting-type activities and be acceptable for moderate-level Riding Club activities but they will never excel in jumping, endurance or dressage

A long humerus with the other necessary conformational attributes, will help a horse to do well in racing, dressage and jumping. Because its angle will set its lower end (the elbow) under or, preferably, in front of the highest point of the withers, there is usually a good front accompanying it, with all its advantages of extension, scope and freedom of movement.

The withers

The best withers for a horse are moderately well defined and long from front to back, running smoothly into the neck at the front and the back behind. As ever good withers provide good attachment for muscles and various important soft tissues and certainly help to keep a saddle in place and steady.

Horses with low withers (usually those of draught-horse blood and also many cobs and native ponies) always present problems in this respect but so do those with exceptionally high withers. Low withers provide no 'anchor' for a saddle which will always have a tendency to slip around to the side no matter how excruciatingly tightly the horse is girthed up (*not* a recommended practice). Such horses frequently have no natural girth groove behind the elbow to act as a bed for the girth, which makes matters worse. However, I regularly ride a cob with virtually non-existent withers and we seem to manage well enough. Many native ponies have this feature, too, but just because it is so common that does not mean that one should not try to avoid it when purchasing a mount.

High, sharp withers also present problems in saddle fitting but they are often made to appear worse because people think they need a narrow saddle, often with a high or cut-back pommel, to accommodate them. In practice, applying a narrow saddle to such a horse often causes too much pressure on the muscles just below and behind the withers (the trapezius and latissimus dorsi muscles, and the longissimus dorsi muscles beneath them) which compresses the muscle tissues there and flattens the blood vessels running through them. Over time, this significantly reduces the circulation of blood through the muscles, obviously, and because the muscles are compressed (and adapt to the pressure, like a finger which always wears a ring) and are also denied an adequate source of nutrients, oxygen and waste removal, they shrink or atrophy, resulting in marked hollows in this area. People then buy narrower and narrower saddles to 'fit' the horse, making the problem worse and worse.

If these horses are fitted with wide enough saddles, often temporarily padded out underneath, and given remedial work in hand or under a properly fitting saddle, the muscles come back to life and the horse develops a normal, natural shape, much to the surprise of the owner. Not all horses with high withers suffer from this problem, although very many do, in my experience. With any high-withered horse – and it is a far less troublesome defect than very low withers – the important thing is to avoid pressure on the top of the withers, as ever, but to fit a wide enough saddle to avoid making the problem worse.

The chest

A good width of chest is shown when the horse's forelegs run vertically down from it and there is room between the front hooves for another hoof. Usually such a horse looks in proportion with a chest neither too wide nor too narrow. A wide chest may seem advantageous for lung and heart room but it is often also shallow. If certainly makes for an uncomfortable, rolling gait and therefore often causes the horse to place more force on each foreleg with each stride.

A narrow chest often causes the forelegs to be too close together or else base-wide (see below). This defect is often associated with poor lung capacity and weakness when it comes to athletic pursuits and is only passable for light to moderate pleasure work. This is one conformational defect which may be brought on to the horse by malnutrition and lack of correct work, resulting in poor muscle development, and it often improves once the horse is managed and schooled properly.

The forelegs

The legs should appear naturally vertical whether seen from front or back, forming a right angle with the ground. *Any* deviation from this conformation is a defect and will cause excess stresses on some part of the leg, so I shall only mention the most common deviations for interest.

From in front, an imaginary vertical line dropped down from the point of shoulder should pass through the centre of the forearm, the knee, the cannon bone, the pastern and the hoof and end at the toe on the ground. Most horses will not quite meet this perfect standard so at least ensure that any slight faults are symmetrical on each leg and that all the leg parts are on the same vertical axis ('facing the same way') so that at least even forces will be felt and the horse is more likely to stay sound.

A horse who stands base narrow will have his feet inwards of the vertical line and will probably go pin-toed or pointing his toes slightly inwards, with some risk of interfering. There will also be greater compression on the insides

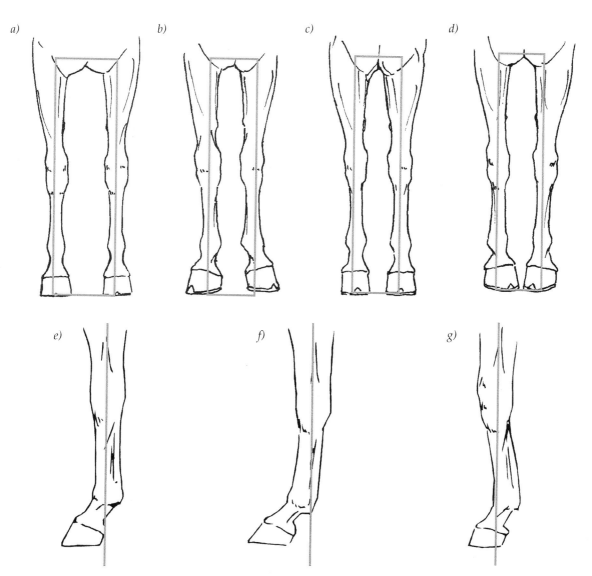

a) Strongly-built, 'straight' forelegs dropping vertically from the points of the shoulders and with enough width between the hooves to take another hoof

b) Toeing out. Horses who toe out sometimes dish in action

c) Bench knees, particularly the right. The cannon should run directly down from the middle of the knee and not be offset to the side. This diagram also shows the conformation known as base narrow where the forelegs and feet are too close together, although it is slight in this case

d) Toeing in. Horses who toe in often plait, bringing one foot in front of the other in action and so having a tendency to trip themselves up

e) Straight foreleg with the cannon forming a directly vertical line under the forearm

f) Back at the knee or 'calf knee' in which the cannon appears to slope forwards and down from the knee. This places considerable extra stress on the back tendons and ligaments of the lower leg which is a serious weakness in any horse used for work or breeding

g) Over at the knee, or 'bucked knee'. This conformation, if very slight, is regarded as an actual advantage by many horsemen as it places less stress on the tendons and ligaments behind the cannon and knee. However, if marked, as here, it can result in the knees buckling in action and in the horse falling. It is not a stable conformation

of his legs than the outsides. If he stands base wide, the opposite will probably apply. The effects of both these faults are increased if the legs are not symmetrical, say with knees or feet rotated inwards.

Bow legs occur when the knees are not bisected by the line but are outside it, whereas knock knees are, obviously, inclined inward. Again, uneven forces equal excess pressure.

Bench knees are not uncommon and occur when the cannon bone below the knee is set to the outside of the knees, placing extra weight on the inside (medial aspect) of the cannon. Offset knees show the opposite, inward set of the cannon, with more stress on its outside (lateral aspect).

From the side, an imaginary line should be dropped from the centre of the shoulder through the forearm, knee and cannon bone, through the fetlock and meet the ground just behind the heel. The most common defect is back at the knee or calf knees in which the knees appear to bend backward so that the leg looks backwardly concave. This is a weak structure which stresses the back of the joint and the tendons and

ligaments, and compresses the front of it. Such horses are only suitable for light work without suffering injury.

Horses which are over at the knee actually have strong forelegs because there is less tension on the ligaments and tendons down the back of the leg. The knee bends forward slightly from the vertical line and, in a mild case, would not be a reason for rejecting a horse. If the defect is pronounced, though, the joint is unstable and the horse may be prone to stumbling and falling.

The barrel

The horse's torso or barrel is obviously where the rider sits and around which her legs lie. A well-conformed horse should have what is termed well-sprung ribs and be well ribbed-up and wider behind the leg than around the girth area, where the rider's legs hang. This makes the horse comfortable to sit on yet still provides room for lungs and heart because the ribcage houses them. Generous, well-sprung ribs, which act to expand the lungs by means of their surrounding muscles, promote good breathing and heart function, so a horse with this quality

Also known as being 'slack in the loins', this conformation, 'herring-gutted', often indicates a horse who will be hard to keep weight on, who 'runs up light' (loses condition) when under stress and may not be so physically strong as a better ribbed-up horse. However, with correct gymnastic work and a diet designed for poor doers, these horses can thrive and work well

a)

b)

a) A well-sprung ribcage is fairly rounded (preferably behind the rider's legs!) and indicates plenty of room for heart and lungs to work – provided the ribcage is not also shallow

b) A slab-sided horse has a much more oval ribcage and may feel rather insubstantial to sit on. However, if the ribcage is also deep, it may not detract too much from heart and lung function

should be suitable for any athletic activity, other points permitting.

A good barrel like this provides plenty of room for muscular attachment, helps to stabilise the saddle on the back (accompanied by good withers) and usually runs into wide loins, which are always desirable. A well ribbed-up barrel will permit the width of your hand between the last rib and the point of hip. The under line of the barrel will not run up sharply towards the stifle but be fairly level all the way along unless the horse is thin. This will also indicate ample abdominal muscles, essential for the horse to shorten his under line, support his spine in a strong if slight upward arch and bring his hindquarters and legs underneath him for a safe, correct and 'thrusting' way of going.

A slab-sided horse, on the other hand, may have a deep chest to compensate for the lack of lung and heart room this conformation usually indicates, but is still usually lacking in that department. A very narrow horse does not feel comfortable or secure to ride and does not make for saddle stability. Some people believe that these horses are also not up to much weight because they have less 'substance' and less back area on which to bear the weight of a rider – although much depends on just how much the rider weighs, of course. Riders who are not heavy and who have shortish legs often prefer

these horses and, provided they are not asked to work hard but made as fit as their lung and heart capacity allow, they can often make good mounts for any pursuit up to moderate work level provided they are well ridden and managed.

The opposite of being well ribbed-up is termed being herring-gutted. In such a horse, there will often be more than a hand's width between the last rib and the point of hip and the belly line will slope up sharply towards the stifle. These horses often appear thin, particularly when fit, and are often difficult to keep looking in good condition. The conformation is exacerbated if the horse is not worked properly and taught to use, and therefore develop, his abdominal muscles.

Horses with this type of conformation are often weaker within their frame than more substantial mounts. They are also often quite long in the back and engagement does not come easily to them, even though they may appear to swing the hindlegs forward well and cover ground, because they do so without flexing much at the lumbo-sacral joint. They often tire easily because they do not go properly, and they do not feel particularly comfortable or reassuring to ride. The normal basic schooling and training technique of groundwork which encourages them (voluntarily, not by means of outline-fixing devices) to lower the quarters, neck and head, raise the back (which uses and develops the abdominal muscles) and lift the legs over poles or grids will help significantly to build them up.

The back

The horse's back is obviously vitally important to the rider! The qualities of a good back for almost any pursuit are that it should be of medium length, more or less flat, wide enough for comfortable saddle bearing, well muscled, with the spine neither prominent nor padded with fat so that there is a channel running down it (although I have seen some exceptionally well-muscled High School horses who showed this feature from work). It should also run smoothly into wide, short, muscular loins. With a back like this a horse is well equipped for any activity.

Short-backed horses were once thought to be handy, agile and strong. A short back is obviously strong (a short stick is stronger than a longer one of the same circumference) but short-backed horses often over-reach until well into

maturity because they find it hard to avoid hitting their front heels with their hind toes. Many find twisting and turning difficult and may also not be as agile as a horse with a more normal back as they may be naturally stiffer.

A long back tends towards weakness particularly in the loin area and the horse may be difficult to bring in hand. These horses often have a long, rangy and lurching stride, so they may not make the most comfortable of rides and often carry themselves with their backs down in more of a 'hammock' than a 'suspension bridge' posture, predisposing them to back strain and injury. Whilst a moderately long back is no disadvantage for dressage, a definitely long one should be avoided for any pursuit. Because of the weakness in the loin area, it is also not a good structure for driving as a strong back is needed to transmit the thrust from the hindquarter forward along the spine to the shoulders and collar or breast harness.

A sway back is the term used when the back dips significantly rather than being more or less

A short back may be strong but is not so flexible as a longer one, and may give a slightly jarring ride but not always and can result in the horse frequently over-reaching (treading on his front heels with his hind toes). This can bruise the front heels and lame the horse. Over-reach boots can help but the main prevention is increasing maturity and strength and a correct way of going developed through schooling

A long back is regarded as weak and can result in a rather 'lurching' ride. Long-backed horses are also very often poorly ribbed up. However, many dressage riders prefer a back which is slightly on the long side as they believe it gives greater flexibility on bends

A sway or hollow back which often means constant, if low grade, back pain for the horse. It creates considerable difficulty in saddle fitting as the saddle, unless specially made, will 'bridge' on the back, with most contact being under the pommel and cantle and little under the seat. Because of this, the corresponding areas of the back will come under too much pressure and be bruised

A roach back is raised, usually in the lumbar/loin area, like this. Although a strong shape, it can be very uncomfortable to sit on and may constantly push the saddle too far forward, a bigger disadvantage when the horse also has only moderate withers and no girth groove

flat. It is a weakness because of the posture it forces on the horse and these horses often find engagement very difficult or impossible. This shape of back can also cause difficulties in saddle fitting as most saddles will 'bridge' the back, making most contact behind the withers and in front of the loins; this obviously creates considerable localised pressure in those places whilst the true back area is not carrying its fair share of weight. It is often necessary to pad up the back with special numnahs and pads when saddling such horses. Remedial work in hand and under saddle involving the correct way of going plus pole work will help these horses considerably.

The opposite conformation, when the visible line of the back arches upwards, is called a roach back, and whilst it may be a very strong formation it is extremely uncomfortable to sit on. These horses often have a hard, rough, lurching stride but can often find a useful life in non-riding pursuits such as driving and, in countries where this is still practised, pack work, provided their harness and equipment is carefully padded to avoid pressure on the spine.

The loins

Because the loins are where the back is joined to the hindquarters (sometimes referred to as a horse's coupling), the loins are a most important area of the horse. They should be short and wide for strength and ample muscle-attachment area to the lateral processes of the lumbar vertebrae.

The crucial lumbo-sacral joint, the point between the last lumbar vertebra in the loin area and the front of the sacrum in the croup area, is where most of the flexion in the horse's spine takes place, discounting the neck and tail, and is the joint the horse must flex to bring his hindquarters and legs underneath him for engagement and scope.

On any horse you are assessing, draw an imaginary line from one point of hip to the other, then feel carefully back along the top of the lumbar (loin) area of his spine until you feel a slight, soft dip, before carrying on and feeling hard bone again at the sacrum. That dip is the location of his lumbo-sacral joint and it should be as far forward as possible in relation to your imaginary line between his points of hip – on the line is perfect if rare. This will mean the horse has a short lumbar/loin area for strength and a long sacrum/croup area for leverage. He will be able to flex the lumbo-sacral joint to bring that long sacrum downward and under with a consequent tilting under of the pelvis and hip joints, producing a long, forward-sweeping thrust of the hindlegs – just what you want in an equine athlete.

A close- or short-coupled horse is one with little space between the last rib and the point of the hip whereas a loose- or long-coupled one has the reverse conformation, more than a hand's width there. A very short or close coupling can result in some lack of lateral flexibility whereas a long- or loose-coupled horse may be rather weak in this area. As in so many things, moderation is key.

The hindquarters

These are famously called the 'powerhouse' of the horse because this is where all the forward thrust and surge comes from. A good horse is said to require the head of a duchess and the bottom of a cook, and no horseman who knows his stuff would argue with that. Very good musculature is essential for virtually any horse expected to exhibit a modicum of athletic ability in any discipline.

The hindquarters should not be too flat (stiff and difficult to engage) nor too sloping (often weak and with limited thrust and scope), but should curve moderately in a long, smooth line to the root of the tail, which should be set on level with the back (assuming the latter is normal). They should be wide, long and deep for ample muscle attachment, size and development, 'square' from the back, and with thigh muscles which meet beneath the tail – although a malnourished horse will probably not show this feature. The overall size and shape of the hindquarters should be noted as they can certainly be built up with correct work provided the potential is there.

A very flat croup and hindquarter with a high-set tail makes it difficult for a horse to engage his hindquarters and hindlegs because the pelvis is naturally tilted rather forward at the

top and backward at the base, so the horse is starting with a disadvantage. Such horses are said to be fast because they take rapid, short strides, but they will never have the reach and scope of horses with a moderately sloped hindquarter top line because their hindlegs are often set out behind them. If efforts are not made persistently to try to encourage them to engage and work properly, they eventually suffer significant back pain and incorrect muscle development due to the stress of going with their backs down and their heads and necks up.

A goose-rumped horse suffers from a hindquarter which is short from front to back and slopes sharply from the point of the croup down to the root of his low-set tail. This makes for weakness due to lack of area for muscle attachment and presence, and it often accompanies sickle hocks (see page 123) and a hindleg set too far under the horse, making for an insecure base of support. These horses often seem to be loose-coupled, too.

Some people confuse a goose rump with a jumper's bump, a feature which shows a prominent point of croup but with good hindquarters. A jumper's bump has traditionally been taken as a sign that a horse will be a good jumper because it provides an extra point for attachment of the muscles of the hindquarters, which are among

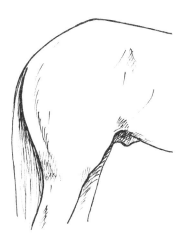

This is a goose rump, not to be confused with a jumper's bump. Goose-rumped horses usually have low set tails and short, poorly-muscled and, therefore, weak hindquarters

those the horse uses for jumping, but very many good jumpers have no such conformation. As we have seen, on post-mortem, horses with jumper's bumps have apparently been found simply to have an abnormal bone formation in this area. However, extra bone means extra muscle-attachment area, so there could be something in this old theory.

The hindlegs

From the back, the hindlegs must appear vertical from the point of the buttock down. Get out your imaginary vertical line, without which we could not manage, and see that it bisects the leg fairly equally from the point of each buttock, the point of the hock and the back of the fetlock. Remember, though, that an absolute, forward-facing angulation of the hindlegs is unnatural and is, in fact, a defect which will overstress the outsides of the legs and feet. The legs from the stifles downwards should point *slightly* outward (with the stifles and feet pointing in the same direction at the same angle) and the points of the

hocks should point *slightly* inward toward each other to the same extent. This is correct, contrary to popular opinion. The important point is that the cannons should be vertical to the ground.

Cow hocks occur when the hocks point towards each other on top of cannons which are nearer together at their tops than at the fetlocks. This is a weak conformation which will compress the outsides of the hock and maybe the fetlock joints. Conversely, bow legs behind, in which the hocks bow outside your vertical line, will be compressed on their insides. Any sign of the horse twisting his hindfeet on the ground in movement is an indication that there is a problem with the angulation of the hindlegs, so investigate this further.

From the side, if you can get the horse to stand naturally absolutely square, with his hindfeet along the same line (neither forward nor back from each other), your imaginary vertical line should drop from the point of the buttock, touching the point of the hock, the cannon and the fetlock, to the ground. This indicates good

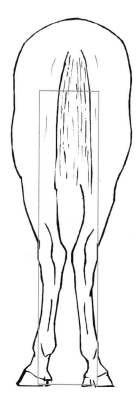

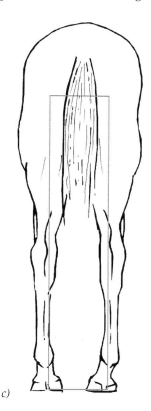

a)

b)

c)

angulation of the joints and a good set or positioning of the hindleg.

In a straight- or post-legged horse, the vertical cannon will come in front of the line and will have a poor ability to absorb concussion because of over-straightened joints. He will also not be able to spring athletically from his hindlegs very well. Conversely, a horse whose hind cannons are vertical but come behind the line is described as camped-out. This is a weaker fault which predisposes the horse to back and hindleg joint strain. He will find engagement difficult, with all its disadvantages.

A sickle-hocked horse's hindleg may be too far back or too far forward, but the identifying feature will be that the cannon will slope down and forward of the vertical, hence the name. This is an even weaker structure which diminishes the horse's ability to push forward strongly with his hindlegs. He would be unsuitable for any power sport such as dressage, jumping, racing or carriage driving but could make a reasonable lightly worked hack or pleasure horse.

The lower leg joints

The point of the hock itself should be sharp and the hock should be big, flat from the sides, cold, hard and 'clean': it is one of the most important joints in the horse's body and any sign of lumps, bumps, softenings, heat or new or old injuries should be discussed carefully with your vet and farrier.

Fetlocks are the most important joints from the point of view of shock absorption and, again they should be flat at the sides, cold, hard and clean. Knees should be big, shield-shaped, flat at the front and deep from front to back. Again, look for any softnesses, rounding of the fronts indicating old injuries, heat, and scarring which indicates a bad fall and perhaps a propensity for falling.

The feet

Feet which are too big are much better than those which are too small. The greater the area over which they can distribute a horse's weight the less force there is concentrated in one small

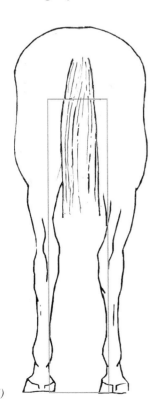
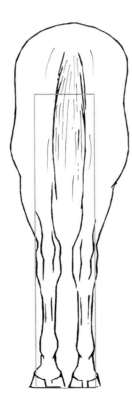

a) Good hindquarters from the back with 'straight' hindlegs and naturally very slightly turned-in hocks and correspondingly out-turned feet – a feature natural to equidae. This is not the conformation known as 'cow hocks'

b) True cow hocks, in which the hocks significantly turn inwards, the hind cannons are not vertical and the hindfeet markedly turn outwards

c) Bow legs in which the hocks are wider apart than the feet and the feet, in this example, are turning inwards to compensate

d) Wide-apart legs which produce an uncomfortable sideways rocking sensation to the gait

e) Close behind. This conformation often results in horses interfering – brushing or speedicutting – and even in their bringing themselves down

d)   *e)*

area. Generally, front feet should be rounded and hindfeet more oval. The walls will angle outwards, and they should be dead straight within that angle, with no cracks or marked ridges which can indicate weakness or disease. The heels should have the same angle as the toe and ideally be about half the height of the hoof at the front wall. From underneath, the feet should appear 'open', not cramped, with well marked bars and frog and with arched soles. Check the hoof/pastern axis.

The effects of conformation on temperament

Anyone who has ever tried to perform some physical act of which he or she is incapable will have a good appreciation of how horses feel when asked to do something for which they are physically unprepared or not equipped. We are now all familiar with the way horses need to go if they are to carry or pull weight safely. Their job is made much easier if, working from back to front in the way they should work themselves, they can flex their lumbo-sacral joints and lower their hindquarters, sweeping strong hindlegs well under their bodies as far as the midline of the belly, and thrust powerfully forward, contract the belly muscles and others around the ribs and under the spine to lift the back, shoulders and withers, extend the shoulders to take the weight of the forehand on spoke-like forelegs, extend the head and neck up and forward from underneath the cervical vertebrae. They should softly accept all this energy and force by flexing the poll (the joint between the skull and the first neck vertebra) and also the joint between the skull and the lower jaw just

below the ear, relaxing the lower jaw. Horses educated and expected to go in this way much of the time are stronger and more resistant to stress and strain than are others.

It is not hard to imagine how discomfort or pain caused by incorrect work or poor conformation can adversely affect a horse's attitude and willingness to co-operate and work with and for us. Horses are very sensitive but also often extremely stoical when it comes to putting up with difficulties. Many of us wish they were not, so that we could know when they have a problem and try to understand it and do something about it. It is vitally important, when choosing a horse for a specific discipline, to pick out the make and shape which will naturally enable him to perform in the way that that discipline demands, and this has been the whole point of this book. Otherwise, we shall, by trying to persuade the horse to work in the required way, put him under unreasonable and unfair stress which may cause discomfort and pain.

In those circumstances, many horses will eventually become resistant and will either withdraw into themselves or actively and sometimes strongly object, when we may possibly label them difficult, bad-tempered, ungenerous or any of several other expressions regularly used to describe horses which are not working as we would wish. Although the horse's basic temperament will not change, his reactions to us and to his work will. Most horses are generous and want to co-operate, trying hard to please, but it must be admitted that a few are not. If at all possible, we should try to find out what the horse's family temperament is like so that we know whether this is just the way he is or whether there is some problem we are causing him by his management and his work.

7

BREEDS, CROSSES AND TYPES FOR THE JOB

It is surprising how very many people in the horse world have strict preferences as to the breed or type of horse or pony they want to be associated with, to ride or work, or to breed. All horses have similar qualities, yet it cannot be denied that many people are irresistibly drawn to specific breeds.

Breeds were created by humans to embody particular qualities that we wanted in our horses or ponies for fun or work. The different physical and temperamental features shown by the different types, and how these evolved, were discussed in Chapters 1 and 2. Now, in this final chapter, I would like to look at just a few of the best known or most noteworthy man-made breeds – those which are most representative of their breed group or type – and at the kinds of work they might be best fitted for. I shall restrict myself to just some of the breeds most likely to be found in the Westernised world and I hope I may encourage you to investigate the subject more thoroughly so you appreciate just what you are dealing with, with every horse you handle.

Far from being an anachronism, the horse seems to be becoming more and more popular as a leisure animal, but let us not forget the finding by the International League for the Protection of Horses mentioned earlier, that of the approximately 122 million horses in the world (excluding working donkeys) about *100 million* are working animals in developing countries, and their owners and families are totally dependent on them for their survival, and some horses are still used in regional wars.

Wherever he is, to the horse the demands of man mean work. He may be asked to carry arms over the mountains of Afghanistan, to pull a heavily laden cart to market in Indonesia, to race round Chantilly, to prance around the riding hall of the Spanish Riding School in Vienna, to herd cattle in Iberia or the American West, to jump round Hickstead, to plough a field in Poland, to follow the Black and Tans over formidable Irish banks or to take a little child for a gentle saunter in his home paddock. All these jobs need different types of horses or ponies, although some could perform several of them equally well, such is the adaptability of the horse.

Hot, cold or warm?

Horse people tend to describe horses loosely as hot-bloods, cold-bloods or crosses. Today, with the rise in popularity of the continental European warmblood breeds, that word, too, is now part of our familiar terminology, if almost entirely with reference to breeds from that region. Any cross between a hot-blood and a cold-blood is, of course, a warm-blood, probably the oldest of which in modern times is the Thoroughbred/Irish Draught cross in its varying proportions, which was winning competitions long before the spread of the modern (continental European) competition warmblood.

Other undoubted warm-blooded types which are not so called are the ancient Iberians (Lusitanos, Alter-Réals and Andalusians), the Friesians, the Lipizanners and others, including many pony types.

Zoologists, biologists and other scientists, however, may be more inclined to describe the different types according to their appearance or morphology – that is, their form and structure – rather than their genetic composition (the amount of 'hot' or 'cold' blood in them) which is what horse people are really referring to when they talk of hot, cold or warm, even if they do not think of it in that way.

So what breeds are described by lay horse people – non-scientists – as cold-bloods? There are several, including the Shire, the Suffolk Punch, the Clydesdale, the Belgian Brabant, the Ardennais, the Dutch Draught and the Percheron. We would regard such breeds as the Arab, the Thoroughbred, the Caspian, the Akhal-Teké, the Tersk, the Karabakh, the Turcoman, and probably the Barb as hot-bloods, and again there are others. In the warmblood category we would include all the continental European riding horse breeds such as the Hanoverian, the Holsteiner, the Trakehner, the Oldenburg, the Selle Français, the Salerno, the Belgian, Dutch, Danish, Swiss and Swedish Warmbloods and the Polish Wielkopolski and Malapolski, plus the newer, still emerging, American and British warmbloods based on continental European blood. As I have said, we accept as warm-blooded, if not warmbloods, any cross between hot and cold, as in most family or pleasure horses and hunters.

There is, of course, one huge category with its own divisions which we have not mentioned yet – the cobs and ponies. Both these types are distinct from horses and from each other and have their own characteristics, and indeed their own character as described earlier. Indeed, it is that indefinable 'pony character' which separates ponies from the others rather than height, which is the technical dividing line (and there is even disagreement over that, some experts regarding anything over 14.2 hands high as a horse and others using 15 hands as the limit). This would place some Arabs and all Caspians and Icelandics in the pony category which they definitely are not, and would mean that many Welsh Cobs and larger ponies such as Highlands were officially horses which, again, they definitely are not.

Horse people understand their own terminologies but I feel that it adds an element of clarity if we also take into account the definitions which might be applied to horses, cobs and ponies by scientists. The terms they might use would be dolichomorphic, mesomorphic and brachymorphic for animals we might describe as, respectively, hot-, warm-, and cold-blooded, although the descriptions do not correlate exactly. *Dolicho* means 'long', *meso* means 'intermediate' and *brachy* means 'short'. Therefore, dolichomorphic-type horses which we would equate with hot-bloods tend to be lightweight and long and lean in the body, and to have long legs, particularly suited to racing and endurance sports. Mesomorphic horses are a little more substantial, with slightly shorter legs, and are suited to general riding, dressage and jumping, light driving and so on. Brachymorphic sorts have short, heavy and muscular necks, bodies and legs and are ideal for heavy haulage, heavy farm work, brewery work and so on. There are two other, self-explanatory, terms which are applied to in-between types – meso-dolichomorphic and meso-brachymorphic which enable us to refine our descriptions further.

Breed 'purity'

In Chapters 1 and 2, the evolution of the horse and the development of types was discussed. It is obvious that, being naturally migratory, the different types, would meet up and mate over millions of years, which is how the basic primitive types evolved naturally and, of course, how breeds and types have been developed by man. This mixing of genes by man has meant that there are no true wild types left in domestication with the arguable exception of Przewalski's Horse (also called the Mongolian Wild Horse), which cannot truly be said to be domesticated but is kept in domesticity for breeding to increase the numbers of this rare breed, and also ferally.

When breed enthusiasts speak of their breed being 'pure' they mean one of two things:

- that the stud book is closed and that no new individuals will be admitted other than those whose pedigrees consist entirely of animals already registered in or traceable to it
- that theirs is a naturally pure breed which has come down to us through Nature, untainted by other genes.

The first definition is fine, but the second refers to something very rare. Probably the 'purest' domestic breeds existing today are the Exmoor Pony, the Icelandic Horse, the Caspian, the Turcoman and possibly some obscure Asian breeds. There is also, of course, the Przewalski Horse.

The breeds described below have been chosen as representative of their type or group and I shall use both lay and scientific terms to describe them. I shall also say what type of work they are best suited for. There are many, many breeds I could have described and I apologise to the enthusiasts of those I have omitted.

The Ardennais/Ardennes

This ancient breed of France has been chosen as typifying the old type of brachymorphic, cold-blooded heavy horse. It is very substantially built, taller than it used to be at 15–16 hands due to infusions of Belgian Brabant plus others, yet it still retains an intriguing, other-worldly air of antiquity about it despite having had its genes tinkered with by man. Its most characteristic colour is strawberry roan. It descends from the prehistoric Forest or Diluvial Horse. There are three types of Ardennais now: the old original type of around 15 hands, the more numerous and bigger, heavier Trait du Nord and the very heavy Auxois which today can really only be regarded as a part-bred Ardennais owing to significant introductions of much other heavy blood.

Suitable/used for: Heavy draught such as short-haul transportation and farm work.

The Percheron

This is a most popular modern heavy horse, again brachymorphic, cold-blooded, but rather different, within its type, from the Ardennais. It is believed to have been founded, intentionally or not, in the eighth century AD by mating Arab and other Oriental horses taken as booty from the Saracens after their defeat at the Battle of Poitiers. Its Oriental ancestry can be seen today in its face, particularly around the eyes, and its energy, free action and relatively clean legs support this. There is a range of types and heights, from 14.3–18 hands or so.

Suitable/used for: Heavy haulage by breweries and forestry concerns, in farming and even, in the lighter types, for heavyweight riding horses. It is, not surprisingly, an excellent foundation breed for the creation of warmblood riding horses.

The Andalusian

Known in Spain as the *Pura Espagnol* (pure Spanish Horse), the Andalusian is increasingly sought-after because of the explosion of interest in classical equitation, but their fairly sparse numbers put their prices out of reach of most potential owners. The Spanish, understandably and wisely, are also reluctant to export their best horses, unlike some countries (particularly Britain), which in the past have had their best breeds decimated by the short-term lure of export money at the expense of long-term international competitive success.

Of mesomorphic, warm-blooded type, the Andalusian descends from the indigenous Iberian Spanish horse, the Garrano, and the Sorraia Pony, with Barb and Arab infusions; this beautiful and noble horse has been bred as a breed in its own right for many centuries. During the eighteenth century, heavy-horse infusions took place to introduce more height and weight – an incredible step – and Napoleon and his officers stole many classic Andalusians. But the Carthusian monks rescued the breed by keeping the best of the remainder and carefully breeding them to maintain the qualities of fire, pride, medium weight and substance plus docility. Today, most of the best horses trace back to Carthusian lines.

Suitable/used for: Bull-fighting, classical High-School, Gineta riding, light carriage work, parade and display work. They have the power and conformation to make good jumpers (like their blood brothers, the other Iberian breeds), being compact, well balanced, athletic and sturdy.

A Lusitano with similar qualities of temperament and conformation to its cousin and fellow Iberian, the Andalusian. (Photo: Peter Sweet)

The Hanoverian

This is probably most people's idea of the quin-tessential warmblood. It is a mesomorphic to meso-dolichomorphic type, depending on the amount of Oriental genes an individual contains and has been painstakingly bred to meet today's competition-horse demand for a quality, athletic horse with scope and substance and a proud but equable temperament. Like the other continental European warmbloods, it has been 'bred up' from indigenous heavy horses and ponies, with infusions of many other breeds and types including Iberian, Thoroughbred, Cleveland Bay and Arab.

The early types were used as warhorses in the Middle Ages, then as heavyish coach horses (if not as heavy as their ancestor, the Holsteiner) but as roads improved and more speed was demanded, the breed became lighter. The post-war leisure horse industry produced today's superb riding-type Hanoverian.

Suitable/used for: Competitive dressage and showjumping are its specialities, also general riding and some carriage driving. Like most continental European warmbloods, it rarely has the speed and toughness for cross-country jumping such as eventing.

The Selle Français

The Selle Français is France's competition warm-blood (although the country's Anglo-Arab could also be described as such, having had some indigenous blood in its early days). It was devel-oped specifically for showjumping and in this has experienced many international successes. There are dolichomorphic and mesomorphic types within the one breed and they range from 15.1 to over 16 hands. It is mainly docile and willing, with the power and athleticism needed for showjumping.

Suitable/used for: Specifically showjumping although, unlike many continental European warmbloods, it is also good at cross-country

and eventing and makes a very good hunter. It races in non-Thoroughbred races in France on the flat and over fences. Needless to say, it makes an excellent general riding horse.

The Thoroughbred

This must surely be the most famous breed in the world, despite being specialised entirely for racing. It is a dolichomorphic type of horse yet cannot be termed a true hot-blood because there are many blank spaces in the early years of foundation pedigrees during the eighteenth century which are almost certain to have been heavy-horse and pony mares. The Thoroughbred often throws up some quite 'common' characteristics: some have unmistakable Roman noses and phlegmatic, even lazy, temperaments, some are 17 hands high and more and have big, rangy bodies. Most, though, resemble true hot-bloods with temperaments and physiques to match.

The Thoroughbred is so famous and valuable not only because of its feats on the racecourses of the world, the prices it fetches at bloodstock sales and the huge purses put up in Thoroughbred racing, but also because, being a mixed breed itself, it blends well with almost any breed to create and upgrade others. All continental warmbloods have a lot of Thoroughbred in them these days, especially the Trakehner and the Selle Français and French Anglo-Arab, and so have the most famous harness racers in the world, the American Standardbreds, plus many others.

Famously descended from three so-called Arabian sires, it is pretty obvious that only one of these was what we would call an Arab today (the Darley Arabian); the Byerly Turk was almost certainly an old Turkmene (an ancestor of the modern Turcoman) and the Godolphin Arabian or Barb was a Barb if his contemporary portraits are anything to go by. This mix of Oriental plus indigenous and imported heavier English and other stock has produced a superlative athlete.

This 26-year-old Thoroughbred mare belonging to the author is a typical example of her breed, her poor top line being purely due to decreased ability to maintain muscle tone due to old age. She is obviously not in hard work, hence the notable grass belly. She was put down due to osteoarthritis in her hocks and hind fetlocks some weeks after this photograph was taken

Suitable/used for: Racing first and foremost, both on the flat and over fences, also eventing, showjumping, hunting, general riding and sometimes dressage, although its normal, long and low action, with little knee lift, would usually preclude it from advanced airs. There have certainly been exceptions, however.

The Arabian

This is one of the most popular breeds, yet many people hate them! The Arab and many of its close crosses have very independent spirits and will not give in to or co-operate with brutes, idiots or control freaks. With owners who wish to be their friends and guiding hands, they will give their all and are fiery yet docile and affectionate.

Claimed by its proponents to be an ancient, 'pure' breed, the Arabian is almost certainly a blend of several ancient hot-blooded types. It can be dolichomorphic or meso-dolichomorphic in type, and is hot-blooded. It shows lean, long-legged racing types (said to be of the Managhi or Muniqui strain like the Darley Arabian) and also slightly more substantial, harmonious types such as the Seglawy and Hamdani strains, all within the same modern breed.

It probably originated from the natural mating of Asiatic and eastern European hot-blooded types which were spread around ancient civilisations. Mohammed's adoption of them in Arabia was a relatively recent chapter in their history and the reason we call them Arabians.

Suitable/used for: A good balanced Arab of riding type (as opposed to the more flimsy, fashionable type often seen in the show ring) is capable of almost anything. Their forté is undoubtedly endurance riding as they have tremendous stamina, but they have always been used for racing, as they are today. They make excellent general riding horses and family horses if handled with sympathy and sense. They can jump quite well, enjoy cross-country work and perform well in dressage if ridden and judged by people who understand their conformation and action – which is that of a real 'daisy-cutter', with little knee bend.

There is barely a breed in the world which does not have at least a dash, and often a lot more, of Arab blood as, particularly before the advent of its descendant the Thoroughbred, the Arab was the first choice for adding quality and riding characteristics to other breeds, and it is still regarded by many as the riding horse *par excellence*.

The Welsh Cob

This is the largest of the four Welsh types and a good specimen is a truly impressive animal.

There is no upper height limit but the best seem to be around 15 hands. A cob of mesomorphic type, which horsemen would call warm-blooded, some are pretty substantial and one of their traditional uses was for light farm work on their native Welsh hill farms.

A true ride-and-drive animal, the Welsh Cob is very compact, well balanced, sturdy and strong. It has come down to us in its present form from the eleventh century and contains original Celtic Pony and Welsh Mountain Pony blood, Iberian, Hackney, some Cleveland Bay from the Yorkshire Coach Horse (now extinct) and some Oriental blood.

Suitable/used for: Ride-and-drive, light farm work, general riding, competitive driving, hunting and also cross-country and showjumping at local level, having good jumping ability.

The Exmoor Pony

This is certainly one of the purest breeds today and a direct descendant of the Celtic Pony; it has no known infusions of other blood. It is unmistakable with its ancient lines, protruding 'toad' eye, brown coat and mealy (beige) colouring on the muzzle and eyes, inside the flanks and under the belly, with no white anywhere. Ancient cave paintings depict the modern Exmoor Pony type! A mesomorphic type, it defies any other modern categorisation, being a truly primeval gift to its present-day enthusiasts. Its numbers are far from generous and everything should be done to preserve and promote its breeding.

Suitable/used for: Endurance riding, because of their tremendous stamina (they can easily carry an adult), competitive driving and as wonderful children's ponies and teachers. The top height is 12.3 hands.

The Irish Draught

This superb horse has traditionally been used to cross with the Thoroughbred and recross to

A truly wild type of Exmoor Pony, which is unmistakable due to its 'toad' eye (obscured here by the generous forelock), the mealy-coloured muzzle and primitive, cold-climate body type. The Exmoor is one of the purest breeds left today and a direct descendant of the primeval Celtic Pony. (Photo: Mike Roberts)

produce some of the best competition (specifically jumping) horses in the world, particularly at the $^7/_8$ TB $^1/_8$ ID and $^{15}/_{16}$ TB $^1/_{16}$ ID proportions. Crosses with more Irish Draught are excellent national cross-country horses and hunters.

Developed by farmers as a general-purpose heavy to light draught horse for farm and other work, both ride and drive, it was originally a meso-brachymorphic type but is now more mesomorphic and warm-blooded. It is stocky, reliable and well balanced with a fair degree of variety within the breed. Indeed, to meet the demands of the current competition market, many Irish Draughts now contain up to a quarter Thoroughbred blood whilst still being registered as full Irish Draught. Based on the Celtic Pony and other indigenous Irish stock, it also contains European heavy blood, as well as Spanish (traditionally from horses washed up from the Spanish Armada as it limped home), Oriental and Thoroughbred.

Suitable/used for: Medium- to heavyweight riding, as a hunter, for ride-and-drive, light farm and draught work and as breeding stock for hunters and competition horses.

A modern type of Irish Draught, of lighter build and more expansive action than heavier, earlier types (which are still readily available) due to the infusion of Thoroughbred blood to meet the demands of today's competition-horse market

The Norwegian Fjord Pony

This larger pony (up to 14.2 hands) is an obvious direct descendant of the mesomorphic Prze-walski Horse with its dun body colour, distinctive erect mane and dark stripe running from the poll all the way down the dock. It also contains Celtic Pony and Tarpan, an Oriental, primitive, dolichomorphic type extinct in its pure form but existing in a 'reconstituted' type in Polish feral herds. The Fjord is mesomorphic in type and could be described as warm-blooded because of its Tarpan ancestry.

It was the mount of the Vikings and has been the traditional pony of Norway for thousands of years. It is depicted on Viking runestones and in other places and its blood has been passed on to various of the world's other pony breeds, not least Britain's Highland Pony and the Icelandic Horse.

Suitable/used for: Riding and driving, mountain work as they are very sure-footed, light ploughing on thin soils, trekking, endurance, competitive driving and trotting races. Strong and willing, some can be stubborn.

The Standardbred

This is the most famous and the fastest harness racer in the world. It paces and trots and is a very impressive animal at work. Bred specifically to race in harness, many do not make comfortable riding horses. A horse of dolichomorphic type, it is truly warm-blooded, being descended from the English Thoroughbred with Norfolk Roadster and Hackney, introduced North American trotting and pacing types and Morgan (itself a mixed breed and one of the most popular in America).

Ranging from about 14.2 to 16.1 hands, the Standardbred is tough and courageous with plenty of character and a normally good temperament.

Suitable/used for: Bred exclusively for harness racing, Standardbreds of suitable conformation take part in endurance riding (having great stamina and guts), hunting, general pleasure riding and even eventing, despite lacking a little speed at the cross-country canter/gallop, as do continental European warmbloods.

The American Saddlebred

A horse of undoubted dolichomorphic type, it is also warm-blooded, elegant, loving and very beautiful. Bred specially to be a quality riding horse with a more equable temperament than the Thoroughbred, it originated in the southern states as a working horse for plantation riding and general 'getting about'. It was developed by interbreeding imported English and European trotting and pacing types, the Narrangansett and Canadian pacers, the Morgan and the Thoroughbred (the previous breeds having Thoroughbred in them, too).

It is one of the famous American five-gaited horses, although some are three-gaited, and is ridden in the American Saddle Seat described earlier. It is so kind it can be handled and ridden by children despite its average height of 15.3 hands, but still possesses the fire and presence needed for a flashy show-ring performance.

Suitable/used for: Specialised Saddlebred show classes and fine harness classes although, with normal shoeing and correct training, it can hold its own with any other breed of riding and competition horse. Its popularity in other fields is restricted by the fact that its tail is usually nicked and set into an artificial carriage (an illegal practice in most countries on humane grounds) and the feet grown long and even built up to encourage high action.

The American Quarter Horse

The fastest horse in the world over 400 m ($1/4$ mile), this is a mesomorphic, warm-blooded type of horse, compact and with chunky muscling definitely of the fast-twitch, anaerobic variety. It was developed by early settlers in America to race down the straight main streets of their towns, which were about 400 m in length, and also in similar-length clearings in the dense primeval forests, hence its name.

It is made up of old Iberian breeds and various early imported European types, Arab, Barb and Thoroughbred; like other American types, selective breeding with these genes has made the Quarter Horse into a recognisable type and breed. Modern Quarter Horses are larger than the early types at 15–16 hands.

Suitable/used for: Sprint racing, cutting, rodeo, trail riding and as an all-round family and general riding horse under saddle and in harness. It also seems to suit and enjoy polo and showjumping, having the agility and power for both sports.

INDEX